The DDP Guide to
Healing Childhood Trauma

THE DDP GUIDE TO HEALING CHILDHOOD TRAUMA

A Visual and Creative Companion for Parents and Practitioners

KIM S. GOLDING

Illustrated by **Juliet Young**

Jessica Kingsley Publishers
London and Philadelphia

First published in Great Britain in 2026 by Jessica Kingsley Publishers
An imprint of John Murray Press

1

Copyright © Kim Golding 2026

Artwork Copyright © Juliet Young 2026

A CIP catalogue record for this title is available from the
British Library and the Library of Congress

ISBN 978 1 83997 824 1
eISBN 978 1 83997 825 8

Printed and bound in Great Britain by TJ Books, Padstow, Cornwall

Jessica Kingsley Publishers' policy is to use papers that are natural, renewable and recyclable
products and made from wood grown in sustainable forests. The logging and manufacturing
processes are expected to conform to the environmental regulations of the country of origin.

Jessica Kingsley Publishers
Carmelite House
50 Victoria Embankment
London EC4Y 0DZ

www.jkp.com

John Murray Press
Part of Hodder & Stoughton Ltd
An Hachette Company

The authorised representative in the EEA is Hachette Ireland, 8 Castlecourt
Centre, Dublin 15, D15 XTP3, Ireland (email: info@hbgi.ie)

Contents

Introduction: Welcome to Our Book

I have had you, the readers, with me throughout the writing of this book. My hope is that I will accompany you as you read and explore the ideas, images and stories. Imagine me by your side as we have a conversation about supporting children with experience of relational traumas, and as we look at the illustrations created by Juliet Young especially for us.

> 'Let's sit side by side and explore how we support children impacted by relational traumas.'

SO, WHO ARE WE?

As I write this introduction, I am aware of you, the reader, and wonder who you are. Where in the world are you living? Where did your ancestors live? What is your identity and what experiences have you had in your life?

I wonder too, what has brought you to pick up this book?

I imagine some of you are parents, drawn to this book because you have experience parenting children who have experienced relational traumas. There are many paths to parenting children impacted by relational traumas. Perhaps you are a birth parent looking for different ways to connect with your child who is experiencing some challenges in the world. Or, maybe you have adopted, are fostering, or are providing respite for a parent who is struggling. Maybe you are parenting within a residential home or offering a home to a birth relative.

Others of you will be practitioners working within health, education, social care or the voluntary and independent sectors. You are supporting children impacted by relational traumas and their families. Maybe you are looking to refresh your understanding or seeking some new thoughts and ideas that can influence your practice.

And of course, many of us are both of these.

In writing this book, I have tried to hold all of you in mind. Inevitably, parts of this book will feel more or less relevant for you depending on your own unique experience and interest. My hope is that you will all find something of value within these pages.

I'm a mother, wife, clinical psychologist, dyadic developmental psychotherapy trainer and author. I was brought up in England, very much a child of the Western world.

I studied, trained and work within a psychological framework embedded in Western psychological thinking and research. To those of you who share this heritage, you will find this influence in my writing and in my stories familiar. To those of you outside this experience who find it less familiar, I welcome you. I apologize if my Western influences are harder for you to recognize. I invite you to find images and stories that represent your experiences.

DEFINITIONS OF TRAUMA

As you may be aware, relational traumas refer to traumatic experiences from within relationships that have the potential to impact the child. This is also called developmental trauma in recognition of the negative impact this trauma can have on the child's development. I use these terms interchangeably.

INTRODUCING DDP

I bring to this book my knowledge and experience of the dyadic developmental psychotherapy parenting and practice (DDP) model, developed by Dan Hughes. This is my guide to approaches that are helpful in supporting the children.

You may have other helpful models in mind, Theraplay, non-violent resistance (NVR), Eye Movement Desensitization and Reprocessing (EMDR), trauma-focused cognitive behavioural therapy, sensory interventions, among others. While I will not be focusing on these here, I know that the DDP model can stretch to embrace them, when appropriate. It does this while offering a relational way of being that informs all this work. If you are using other models, I am confident you will find ways of making these work together.

For those of you unfamiliar with the DDP model, here is a brief summary.

DDP is a relational model that offers a range of approaches to help children impacted by relational trauma, their families and the practitioners supporting them. As we will explore, while DDP began as a therapy it has expanded to also provide parenting and network support.

All these approaches are provided based on the same principles:

- Healing from the impact of relational traumas involves experiencing healthy relationships, especially with parents.
- The child will mistrust these relationships, find ways to avoid emotional connection and to resist what the parent is offering.
- We offer the child a PACE attitude in which they experience the other *accepting* (A) their experience, holding *curiosity* (C) for this experience and providing *empathy* (E) for the child's worries and fears alongside a genuine enjoyment in the relationship which is light and *playful* (P) when appropriate.
- This provides the child with different relational experiences that helps them to move from mistrust to trust in being parented.
- These different relationships offer attachment security. This means that the child experiences the parent(s) to whom they are emotionally attached as offering a safe base from which they can explore the world.
- These relationships also offer healthy intersubjective experiences.

'Intersubjective' is a technical term to capture the idea that we share our subjective experience within relationships. In other words, our internal experience of feelings and thoughts is shared within the relationship, influencing each other and the way the relationship develops. The emotional connection that this provides helps the child to learn about themselves, others and the world.

Children who have experienced unhealthy or neglectful intersubjective experience and insecure attachments resist these relationships, demonstrated through controlling behaviours.

Through a PACEful presence, the parent over time helps the child to develop increased security and become more open to the intersubjective experiences being offered to them. The controlling behaviours reduce, and the child is more open to the influence of the parent.

The child then has the safety to make sense of their current experience, including their doubts and worries about self and others, in the light of their past experience.

As the child understands their story, they can be supported to grieve the losses they have experienced and to heal from the trauma. This leads to a transformed sense of self and increased trust in supportive others.

> 'The foundation of DDP provides a place of safety within which parent and practitioner support the child to heal and thrive.'

I hope that this summary helps you to recognize how key safety is for everyone when helping children recover from the impact of relational traumas. The DDP practitioner is vigilant to threats to a sense of safety. These may be because of past trauma, including transgenerational trauma, or current experience, including intersections with oppression, marginalization and discrimination.

When safety is lost, the priority becomes finding ways to return to a sense of safety. The provision and restoration of safety allows the child and family to begin the process of healing from the impact of relational traumas.

We will explore how this leads to DDP approaches which can provide co-regulation and co-creation of the child's experiences, current and past.

Co-regulation refers to the way we can help children (and each other) to manage feelings when they grow big and threaten to overwhelm. Co-creation refers to reflecting on and making sense of experiences together.

This co-regulation and co-creation of the child's experiences facilitates the transformation of the child from one who holds fragmented stories of shame and terror leading to isolation and self-loathing to the discovery of stories of connection, strength and resilience.

You may be thinking that this is easy to write but hard to envisage. Stay with me and together we will dive into these ideas and explore what they look like in practice. In this way, we can all play a role in helping the child to learn to trust in others, trust in themselves and trust in the future.

PARENTS AND FAMILIES

A quick reflection on the words 'parent' and 'family'. I use these words throughout the book, and I do want you to feel at home in this language.

For 'parent' I am considering anyone who has a parenting role for the child. This might be parents within a traditional Western nuclear family, but it equally applies to parenting within communities.

Family is equally broad. It is the community around the child who has an interest in helping the child grow and develop to fulfil their potential.

Within this book we will meet birth parents alongside those who come to parenting via fostering, adoption or kinship care. We will also meet residential homes, where the whole residential team provide a family for the children in their care, and give thought to community leaders who provide guidance and support.

> 'Parents, family and community all play a role in supporting our children.'

THE INFLUENCES ON THE DEVELOPMENT OF DDP

The development of DDP has been influenced by Western-informed theories of attachment, intersubjectivity and neuroscience. Although founded in these, in the context of a culture of individualism and achievement, DDP has people at its heart. It has a focus on family and community support. In its emphasis on listening, witnessing, story-telling and trusting in self-healing, the influence of indigenous cultures can be seen. My hope and endeavours are that these move us beyond the narrow views held in the West.

Incidentally, I am not going to spend much time exploring theory. There are many books about DDP that do that in depth. Here I want us to explore the practice.

DDP approaches rely on supporting families with an open and engaged stance which holds curiosity about the child and family. The

DDP practitioner is interested in the other's experience. This might be their culture, religious beliefs, class, sexuality, gender identity, health and neurodiversity. Approaches are tailored to the unique needs of the people we interact with.

DDP was developed in the West but is applicable around the world. Wherever you live, whatever your heritage, I welcome you to join us in this development.

> 'Together we can develop a model fit for the future.'

SPACES WITHIN THIS BOOK

I also want to welcome readers with neurodiverse needs. I am a creature of words. I can be absorbed by them for hours. I have tried to write this book in a way which is accessible to those who find reading trickier, or whose attention needs gaps and spaces.

To help with creating spaces, I have included *'reflection moments'*. I want to have a conversation with you. This is tricky when we are in different times and places from each other. I hope that these reflection moments help. We can slow down (a favourite idea within DDP!), while we explore together. I invite you to join me in these reflections, while knowing that we each have our own ways of engaging with a book.

At the end of each part, I have included some *'reflection pages'* to give you another opportunity to pause and reflect. I invite you to use these for your own notes, stories and images.

> 'Through moments of reflection, you will join me in creating this book.'

STRUCTURE OF THIS BOOK

For those of you who like structure, here is a brief plan of the book.

The book is divided into 40 short chapters, in five parts. Within each chapter I have written some notes about pivotal ideas within DDP, Juliet has created an image, and I have written a story or narrative verse.

Part 1: What Is DDP? Here we explore some of the foundational ideas behind DDP approaches. We go on a journey into safety and vulnerability. We explore trusting the process and the importance of relationship. We understand how relational traumas can lead children to fear others, and the power of storytelling within emotionally connected relationships. We recognize the influence of the past on the present, and the sense of shame that can arise.

Part 2: PACE: The Therapeutic Attitude. This takes us into a deeper exploration of how an attitude of playfulness, acceptance, curiosity and empathy helps us to emotionally connect. We consider each element of PACE and how they work as a whole.

Part 3: DDP-Informed Parenting. Therapy for children is most beneficial when it is supported by DDP-informed parenting. This section explores the power and challenge of staying open and engaged when parenting children, alongside providing the guidance, supervision and discipline that is needed. This is summed up in the phrase 'two hands of parenting'.

Part 4: DDP-Informed Parenting Support. This part reflects on the challenges of parenting children impacted by relational traumas. We focus on the potential impact this has on the parents and how practitioners can help. We also discover the importance of 'modelling the model' to help others in their way of being.

Part 5: DDP in Therapy. We end where DDP began, reflecting on the therapeutic work with the child. DDP language shines through as we explore the structure of a DDP session and the power of storytelling and witnessing.

'So, let's get started.'

Part 1

WHAT IS DDP?

You may be parenting a child who has experienced relational traumas or supporting these children as part of clinical, education or social care practice. If so, it's likely that you will be trying to find ways to relate to your child or children – to help them to feel safe, to trust and to heal from the negative impacts of the traumas they have experienced.

Let's have the first of our 'reflection moments' together.

REFLECTION MOMENT

★ When you think about the child or children you are parenting and supporting, what do you want from an intervention model?

Of course, we all want children to heal, to be healthy, to achieve. We have a desire to 'fix' children in some way. I want to extend your thinking beyond this. Instead of 'fixing', let's think about finding ways to provide the children with environments within which they can thrive.

Trying therapy, which helps children to grow strongly from their trauma, is a part of this, but there is so much more that we can offer these children. You will have a role to play in this, and the DDP model has much that can help you in this work.

SO, WHAT IS DDP?

Think of DDP as a therapeutic model of many parts. It describes a range of approaches to help children who have experienced relational traumas, as well as their families and the practitioners supporting them. We will mainly be focusing on the parenting and therapy parts in this book.

DDP was developed by Dan Hughes, a clinical psychologist in America. It was the late 1980s and Dan wanted to find a way of helping the children and foster/adoptive families he was working with at the time. In his experience, the traditional approaches were not helping.

Since those early days, DDP has developed and expanded to involve the following areas:

- **Dyadic developmental psychotherapy:** This was DDP's origins and remains a central feature of the model.

- **Dyadic developmental parenting:** Parents are integral to supporting their child's therapy. They are most helpful when they adopt DDP-informed parenting, so that the child gets a family experience of being bathed in the DDP principles.

- **Dyadic developmental practice:** Parents and children need and deserve support beyond the therapy room. The child needs help in school and the whole family benefit from sensitively provided social care and community support. When practitioners adopt DDP-informed practice, the child experiences joined-up environments informed by the DDP principles.

DDP always sits within a context. This includes the culture, experience and identity of the children, families and practitioners. It is important that this context is explored and considered so that approaches are adapted for the unique child and family. This includes extending beyond developmental trauma to also consider other traumas the child has been exposed to. These might be current traumas, like being bullied in school or not having parts of your identity accepted. They might include past traumas passed down through the generations, such as having ancestors who were relocated, persecuted, enslaved or colonized.

Children with experience of relational traumas are a marginalized group. Many of them have identities and experiences that further marginalize them.

All this 'context' needs to be understood and considered when working within the DDP model.

REFLECTION MOMENT

Reflect on a child who has experienced relational traumas.

★ What traumas has the child been exposed to – directly or through their family history?

As DDP has developed and grown, so has the DDP practice model. Here is an illustration of what the current model looks like.

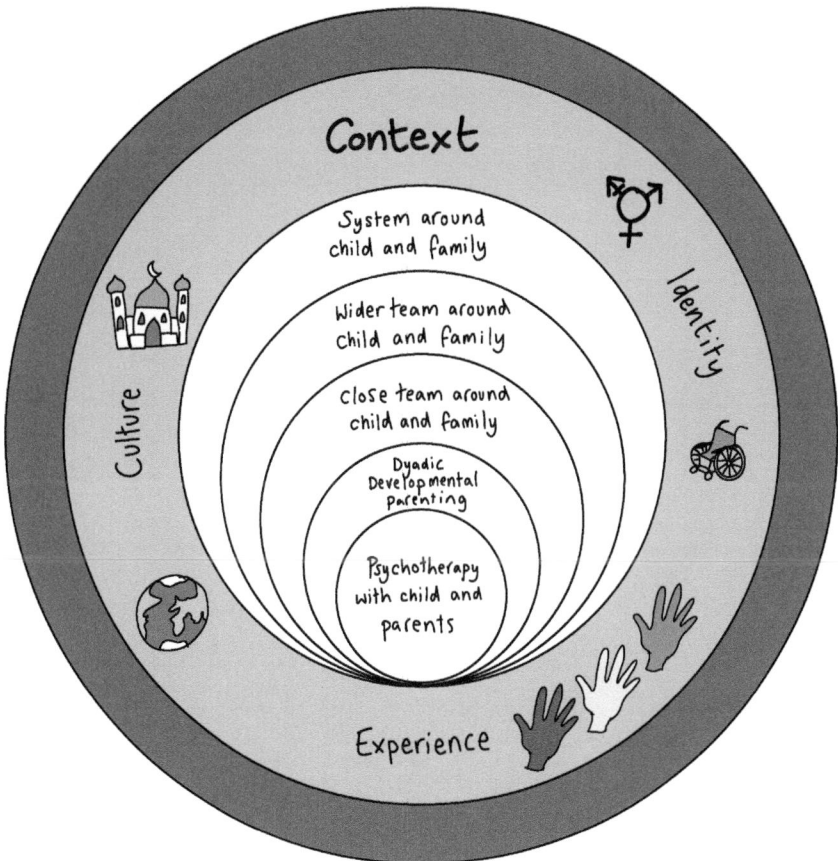

Adapted from *Healing Relational Trauma With Attachment-Focused Interventions* by Daniel A. Hughes, Kim S. Golding and Julie Hudson. Copyright 2019 by Daniel A. Hughes, Kim S. Golding and Julie Hudson. Used by permission of W.W. Norton & Co.

REFLECTION MOMENT

★ Do you see parts of this model that could be helpful to you in your parenting or practice?

As you dip in and out of this book, this model provides you with a map. Maybe it is a map that you can add to as you experience your own way of being within this DDP framework.

1

DDP Focuses on Helping Children and Families to Feel Safe

Of course, we start with safety. This is where children need us to start.

If you were thinking about where safety is located within the human body, where would you place it?

For me, safety is in the core. It sits centrally, giving strength to the spine and helping the head to be erect so it has clear vision. As it moves through the core it comes close to the heart, where I place emotional connection.

As safety is so fundamental it makes sense that we start with safety, and return to its restoration when it is lost.

REFLECTION MOMENT

★ What does safety feel like to you?
★ Where do you experience it within your body?
★ What feels different when you encounter threats?
★ How do you feel safe again?

DDP approaches help children and families to feel safe enough to thrive.

Think about children who experience security in their relationship with their parents. Psychologists describe this as having a secure attachment. How easily can they experience safety in emotional connection?

> 'Safety is where we start and need to return to. Only in safety can we experience comfort and joy.'

The safety of emotional connection is offered in the many intersubjective experiences that the family offers. These are synchronized, shared experiences where each individual is open to the influence of the others. Children learn about themselves from these experiences. As they experience themselves as loveable, they are open to the comfort they require when they need it. When they experience themselves as delightful, they are open to shared moments of joy.

It is very different for children impacted by relational traumas. Their experience leaves them feeling unsafe in emotional connection and resisting intersubjective experiences. They do this by being more controlling in their relationships. Through controlling behaviours they are less open to the influence of the other and this feels safer. These are children described by psychologists as having insecure and disorganized attachments.

REFLECTION MOMENT
Consider how relational traumas lead children to resist emotional, intersubjective connections.

★ Why does controlling others feel safer?

The early experience of relational traumas often leaves children feeling unloveable and not delightful. The children withdraw from reciprocal connections. In controlling others, they are avoiding anticipated dangerous or unpleasant connections. In the process, they lose opportunities to experience comfort and joy.

> 'Do not connect with me. I fear your connections are full of thorns that hurt.'

DDP approaches aim to restore a sense of safety in emotional connection, opening the intersubjective world of relationships to the children.

This is tricky. Having had experience of being hurt in relationships, children don't readily move into new relationships. Even when a relationship is safe and caring, how can the child know this? Hoping it is different this time can feel like a very big risk.

Once you have touched fire and been burnt, would you touch it again, even if told it is now cold?

I DON'T FEEL SAFE WITH YOU

Indira lies in her bedroom listening to the sounds of family below. The events of the school day still resonate.

Another day of being bullied for being 'the foster kid', for looking different, for having joined the school part way through the term.

Another day of being in trouble from the teachers for not focusing, for not producing work, for not engaging with the other children.

Indira lies on the bed not aware of the habitual well of loneliness that surrounds her; not aware of the longing to be part of this family that is buried within her. She is only aware of the need to stay apart, to stay in control, to not let anyone near.

Indira hears the foster mother coming upstairs. Pretending to be asleep, she hopes she will pass by. Hearing her pause at the door Indira pulls the bedcovers over her.

THE FIRST LAYER OF HER ARMOUR TO KEEP PEOPLE AWAY IS IN PLACE.

This mother is persistent. She gently knocks and then opens the door. Indira hears her words. They sound kind, but she's aware that kind words usually have a bite to them. She ignores the questions about her day, the concern about how she's feeling, the invitation to talk or even to join them.

THE SECOND LAYER OF HER ARMOUR IS IN PLACE.

The mother doesn't go away. She sits on the chair across the room and continues talking. Why won't she leave? Indira shouts to be left alone. She shouts words of insult, of abuse. She threatens all sorts of harm to the mother, to the other children, to herself.

THE THIRD LAYER OF HER ARMOUR IS IN PLACE.

And still the mother does not go. She talks quietly to herself. She wonders if the children were mean to her in school today. She wonders if the teachers were cross that she hadn't done her homework. She guesses that Indira has armour in place and how important this is to her. She guesses that Indira needs to be angry, to shout, to threaten and that somewhere inside her she wishes it could be different. She hopes that one day Indira will not need her armour but knows that it is not this day. Indira notices the armour lessen just a little. She notices a sense that maybe she could feel safe here. She still wants her armour close but maybe there is space within it for a tiny fragment of hope that maybe this time will be different.

2

A Way of Being, Each to the Other

We can't move deeply into exploring DDP without running into PACE. This is 'the attitude' that is central to the DDP way of being. The founder of DDP, Dan Hughes, used PACE to capture emotional connection within relationships:

- *Playfulness* conveys enjoyment of the relationship.
- *Acceptance* conveys that your inner world of thoughts and feelings is neither right nor wrong; it simply is.
- *Curiosity* conveys that you don't know but you wonder about the other and what they are thinking and feeling.
- *Empathy* conveys that you understand and feel with the other.

> 'When we all hold PACE, change will happen.'

Have you noticed how when you experience playfulness, acceptance, curiosity and empathy from others, you feel more emotionally connected to them? The attitude helps to build a sense of safety, and builds trust in the relationship.

> **REFLECTION MOMENT**
> Imagine you are talking to an infant. The infant can't understand your words.
>
> ★ What do you think they are experiencing?

Do you think PACE comes easily when we talk to infants? Without expectations of them, without the need for discipline, we can more easily focus on the infant's inner world. It is this understanding and curiosity about the inner world, alongside our enjoyment of the relationship, that builds emotional connection.

REFLECTION MOMENT

Now imagine talking to an older child.

★ Do you notice anything different?
★ How are you connecting with the child?
★ What else are you trying to achieve in talking to this child?

I wonder if you agree with me that PACE is less easy the older the child is. We have many things we want to achieve when we talk to children. We want to guide them with their behaviour and help them to think about others, to achieve in a task, to help with chores, to be nice to friends. The list goes on.

Emotional connection gets diluted with so many things to focus on.

REFLECTION MOMENT

Finally, imagine talking with a friend or colleague.

★ How much time do you spend exploring their emotional world?
★ How much time are you focusing on what has happened, then offering reassurance, problem-solving or simply seeking more information?

While a focus on what has happened is important, problem-solving can be very helpful in leading to solutions, and reassurance has its place if it isn't dismissing the feelings of the other, these actions will only do so much in helping you to understand the full picture.

Using the DDP model, we aim to adjust the balance within relationships. Instead of moving too quickly to offer guidance, reassurance or solutions, we make sure that there is sufficient time spent on understanding the person. Feeling understood, and that the other person gets us, is the emotional connection that helps us to feel safe. It enables us to have trust in our relationships and be open to the support that connections and relationships can offer.

> 'When we are focused on behaviour, it is easy to forget the inner emotional world.'

So, having a playful, accepting, curious and empathic approach (PACE) is an important part of helping children to recover trust and experience safety in relationships.

Each of us sits within chains of relationships. Each relationship within a chain can feel supportive, available and valuing of us. On the other hand, it's possible for any of these to feel unsupportive, unavailable, and not valuing.

These experiences are contagious.

If we feel supported, we have energy to support others.

If we feel valued, it is so much easier to value others.

If people make time for us, we are more inclined to make time for others.

REFLECTION MOMENT

Think of a day when PACE was absent in your relationships.

★ What did the links in your chain of relationships feel like?

Now think of a day when you experienced PACE from others.

★ What did the links in your chain of relationships feel like in that case?

PACE helps us to be supportive: 'I am interested in you and want to understand your experience.'

It demonstrates our availability: 'I am ready to slow down and truly listen without dismissing what you feel.'

It shows that we value and enjoy the relationship we have with the other: 'Let's spend time together.'

Many people have told me how simple PACE sounds, and how hard it is in practice. Perhaps you find the same. If we have been brought up in relationships which are light on PACE, it can feel unnatural to bring PACEfulness more centrally within our relationships. It is something many of us need to work at. I have found it is worth the effort, transforming personal and professional relationships. I hope you do too.

THE LINKS IN THE CHAIN

Think about one link in your chain of relationships – PACE moves backwards and forwards along the chain, forming healthy links.

A headteacher takes the time to notice that one of the teachers in their school has arrived looking stressed. They listen empathically as the teacher describes a difficult issue at home.

The first link in the chain.

The teacher goes into the classroom. The teaching assistant is anxious because the child they are supporting is already showing signs of dysregulation. The teacher spends a moment co-regulating with the assistant.

A SECOND LINK IN THE CHAIN.

The assistant turns to the child offering them the time and space they need to settle into the classroom.

THE CHAIN EXTENDS TO INCLUDE THE CHILD.

At the end of the day the child skips out of school smiling at the teacher and assistant as they pass.

THE LINKS OF THEIR CHAIN ARE STRENGTHENED.

The parent approaches; the teacher gives a little smile of encouragement, 'Your child is okay.'

THE CHAIN LENGTHENS TO INCLUDE THE PARENT.

The parent takes the child's hand. They laugh at the antics of the young lambs in the field and the parent listens empathically as the child, once again, complains at how mean the other children were during breaktime.

PARENT AND CHILD ARE LINKED WITHIN THE CHAIN.

The child lets their sibling have first go on the trampoline without the usual argument.

A CHAIN BEGUN IN SCHOOL ALSO EMBRACES A FAMILY MEMBER.

Today has been a good day.

3

A Relational Approach

DDP is a relational approach. Relationships are central to every DDP approach – whether in therapy, parenting or practice.

> **REFLECTION MOMENT**
> Reflect on the relationships you have.
>
> ★ What is the importance of these relationships?
> ★ Are there any relationships you would rather not have?

I expect that, like me, you will have some relationships you cherish, some relationships you work at and some relationships you could do without!

What would your life be like without any relationships?

We only need to watch an infant to know how important relationships are for human beings. We are born for social connections and infants have innate, sophisticated skills to ensure that these connections happen. Long before infants move around, use language or feed themselves, they are skilled in engaging other humans.

> 'We are born for relationships. Relationships are central to being human.'

Developmental trauma tramples on these innate skills for social connection as the child learns to fear what they are born to need.

REFLECTION MOMENT

★ Do you have ways to manage tricky relationships?
★ Do you avoid them or have ways to make them easier?

As the child impacted by trauma grows, they resist relationships, especially the parenting relationships that have felt so dangerous. This resistance becomes their companion as they move into new families and as they meet caring, supportive adults in their schools and communities. They remain alert to the dangers that all adults might present. This is hypervigilance, as they look out for and imagine signs of dangers. They adopt controlling behaviours to ward off these potential dangers. They cannot relax, learn or play as danger feels ever present.

Hypervigilance and control become the two weapons they wield as they try to protect themselves from the hurt and pain that they anticipate.

'Children hurt in relationships need to heal within healthy relationships.'

Recovering from the impact of any trauma is reliant on the supportive relationships around us. We need relationships we can be vulnerable in, so that we can be supported to process the trauma and thus minimize its impact. We come to understand and integrate our experience of trauma so that it becomes a healthy part of who we are. We develop resilience and flexibility where there was vulnerability and rigidity.

When we are socially isolated, the trauma continues to invade our body, our life, our dreams.

Can you see the dilemma here?

If children need relationships to recover from trauma and yet they also resist these relationships, how can recovery happen?

DDP provides approaches that help children to discover safety in relationship and regain their birth right of social connection.

BORN IN PAIN

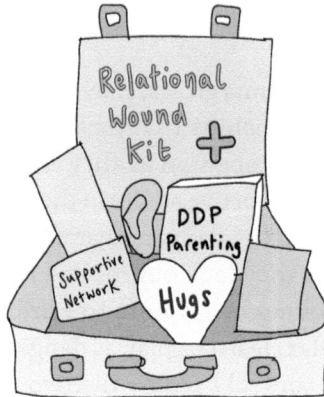

The foetus develops in the warmth of the womb.
But this womb's dark warmth is deceptive.
Their primitive system absorbs toxic substances that feed it.
Their immature hearing absorbs the surround
sound of hate and violence.

The newborn arrives into bright light and loud noise.
This is a world that does not nurture.
The newborn seeks warm hands and kind eyes to soothe their fears.
They find despair in the cruel hands and
loud voices that are around them.

The infant's optimism seeks for what they need.
They turn to those who might offer care.
They cry out to communicate their need for food, warmth and soothing.
They stop crying as they discover a world where these do not exist.

The toddler develops skills to help them survive.
Skills they never should have needed.
They learn to stay still and hide as they disappear into silence.
They learn to shut out the intense pain of living in the world alone.

The child is adopted into a loving home.
They have little shoved in a black bag.
They hold tight to hard-won abilities that help them stay hidden.
Living in the world alone feels safer than living in this family.

The parent shows their kind eyes and loving hands.
The child resists all that is offered.
They mistrust the kindness and fight against the deceptions they fear.
The parent offers care even facing the despair of this rejection.

The therapist offers the parent their kind eyes.
Together they witness the child's pain.
The child hears their story of hurt as the parent offers them love.
The child begins to wonder if after all they are loveable.

Healing has begun.

4

Supporting the Heart and Mind

This chapter introduces some of the DDP language and principles that have emerged during its development. We dip into these here and revisit them later in the book.

All these principles involve emotional connection. Through emotional connection we meet heart to heart and mind to mind.

REFLECTION MOMENT

★ What do you hold in your heart and in your mind?

Does it make sense to you that the DDP approach encourages children to make emotional connections through the heart, while their minds make sense of their current and past experience? We all enjoy being understood, mind to mind.

'To listen fully, DDP listens with heart and mind.'

Dan Hughes reflected on listening fully when he spoke at the DDP conference held in Kansas in 2019:

> To fully listen is to fully respond to the other. Moment to moment. Fully listening leads to being invited into the heart and mind of the other. It enables the heart and mind of the other to affect us deeply – and so affect the other deeply.

> **REFLECTION MOMENT**
> Reflect on what you hold in your heart and mind.
>
> ★ Can you see ways that this helps you listen?

Do you, like me, find that it is unusual to sit and reflect on listening? We learn to listen when we are very young and maybe because of this it is something we rarely think about in depth.

Our main sense for listening is our hearing, but all our senses are involved. In deafness, a person develops their ability to listen using sight and touch beyond anything a hearing person can do.

Listening to another is a complex activity.

> 'In listening to you, I understand you more deeply. I understand what is in your heart and mind.'

DDP principles help us to bring heart and mind together.

Here is my summary:

- *PACE* brings the curiosity of the mind together with the empathy of the heart.

- *Storytelling* allows us to communicate fully via the *affective-reflective (AR) dialogue.*

- *The affect* of the AR dialogue brings the heart, matched to the emotional experience of the other.
  'If you are angry, I will resonate with the intensity of your feelings. If you are sad, I will resonate with the depth of your sadness.'

- *The reflective* of the AR dialogue uses the mind to find words to put to these experiences.

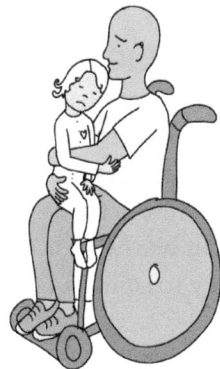

(*with intensity*) 'You are so angry. Of course, you are. If that had happened to me, if I had been let down by my friend, I would be angry too. Why would she do that to you?'

(*in a more subdued tone*) 'It's so sad when friends let you down. I see how much this hurts. You have struggled so much to have friends. I wonder if it leaves you feeling that you shouldn't bother. Maybe you worry that you are not someone who can have friends. How sad is that.'

- *Follow-lead-follow* is a process that helps us to follow where the other leads us. We notice their mind and what they are trying to communicate either verbally or non-verbally. We then lead them deeper into connection with their heart as they feel felt in all that they are experiencing. We then follow again as they respond to our deepening connection with their experience.

- *Talking with, about and for* provides us with different ways to emotionally connect. We talk with the other, together discovering the story that sits in their heart and mind. When this feels too overwhelming, we can talk about them or wonder aloud so that they quietly experience their story being witnessed. When they struggle to find words to describe what sits in their heart, we offer words based on the story we have been discovering together.

- Sometimes our attempts to connect go astray. We notice the *rupture* to the relationship, as hearts and minds become disconnected. We pause, feel with them, and *repair* the rupture so that we move back into connection again.

FINDING HEARTS AND MINDS IN THE THERAPY ROOM

Cassie storms into my room and drops down into the chair. Her adoptive mother follows apologetically behind. My attempts to connect with Cassie land like a stone. I wonder to myself what she is trying to communicate to me with this entrance. I'm not sure what is on her mind but her heart is right there. Matching the intensity of her entrance, I try to connect with this.

Therapist: 'Oh Cassie, I'm sorry. Here am I wondering how you are and you've just shown me! Wow, it sure looks as if something has made you cross today. I'm not sure how much you want to be here just now.'

Cassie (*with 14-year-old sarcasm*): 'Oh dur! You don't say!'

Mum looks at me and shrugs slightly, as she signals, 'Can you deal with her, as I can't?' Cassie catches the movement and responds angrily. She tells her mother to back off as this is her session and she doesn't want her to interfere.

Therapist: 'This is your session, Cassie, and I'm wondering how you want to use it. I'm here. I see you're angry. Can I help?'

Cassie: 'Well, wouldn't you be angry if your best friend had just dumped you and your mother has been on your back all morning. I only forgot to feed the stupid rabbit once. It's not like I killed it or something.'

I notice a slight shifting of mood in Cassie's communication. The anger is still there. I also feel the hurt and the shame that are lying underneath. I want to connect to her words and also to this emotional experience.

Therapist (*moving a little closer*): 'I'm beginning to see, Cassie. It sounds like you've been having a hard time. Your friend has let you down. I see that has made you angry, and I'm thinking how hurtful this is. We rely on our friends and when they're not there for us, it stings. I'm guessing you were so preoccupied with this that you forgot to feed your rabbit. I know how fond of her you are. I wonder if you felt bad when Mum reminded you. This sounds like a lot.'

Cassie is now fully connected with me. She tearfully tells me how her friend had found out who her birth family is and had said very mean things about them to some of the other children at school. I gently explore this with her, recognizing how hurt and let down she feels. I notice the feelings of betrayal and how hard it is to trust in friendship again. Cassie agrees, telling me she's done with friends now. She'll manage on her own.

Cassie then allows me to connect her with the deeper pain of not feeling good enough, not with friends and not with her birth family. She is able to stay with this as I move between talking with her and talking for her when the hurt is too hard for her to put into words. As she leans into her mother, I gently talk, telling her mother the story that Cassie and I have discovered together. It's a story of things going wrong with friends which woke up a bigger hurt of losing her birth family. As her mother looks at Cassie with kind eyes that reflect the empathy she is feeling, I quietly talk for Cassie, capturing her heart and mind with this story of hurt and loss. Cassie's mum responds with acceptance and empathy and also apologizes for getting cross about Cassie not feeding the rabbit. She knows that Cassie loves her rabbit and would never hurt her and she is happy to be back-up carer for the rabbit, as we all forget things sometimes.

As they continue to sit together, I notice out loud how Cassie has a kind heart and loving soul. I reflect on how friends will let us down at times and sometimes parents cannot look after their children for all sorts of reasons. I hope that right here and now, Cassie can experience that she is good enough and she is loved. Cassie gives a little smile as she looks at her mum.

As Cassie and her mum leave my room, calmer and more connected than when they had arrived, I reflect on the power of connecting three hearts and minds and the healing narratives that emerge when we do so.

5

Providing Words for Experience Through Storytelling

I expect you noticed in Chapter 4 how much the DDP principles rely on storytelling. Whether we are telling a fictional story or witnessing a real-life story of the other's experience, we do this with a storytelling tone of voice and rhythm of speech.

> 'Storytelling holds our attention in a way that lectures never do.'

When we want to help a child, we don't want them to feel lectured to or talked at. We want them to be fully engaged in the story of their life. Storytelling helps us to achieve this.

REFLECTION MOMENT
Imagine a world without storytelling.

★ What would be missing?
★ What would be difficult if you couldn't discover someone's story?

It's hard to imagine, isn't it? How would you talk to a friend, teach a child, communicate the wisdom of the elders, share cultural norms and values, read a book, watch a film, offer a healing circle, create a dance, compose music, produce art?

Humans around the world are storytellers. Our ancestors painted scenes from their life on the cave walls in prehistoric times; oral storytelling passed history, culture and mythology from one generation to the next. Writing gave humans alternative ways of preserving these stories and the arrival of printing presses made these more accessible. Technology has added to the ways we communicate through story in many parts of the world.

> **'Humans are born storytellers.'**

We bring this part of our humanity to DDP approaches. DDP conversations are made in a storytelling style which we call affective reflective (similar to the 'affective-reflective dialogue' which was introduced in Chapter 4).

- The *reflective* is the content of the story or narrative that we discover when we read the story.
- The *affective* is the way we talk about this narrative, bringing the emotion of the experience into the telling.

When you reflect on this storytelling style, do you notice how the rhythm, tone and quality of conversation are similar to conversations you might have with a friend over a cup of coffee, even though the content is different?

These conversations can be part of a therapy process, as well as encouraged within the parenting and support of the child.

When the child's attention is held by the adults' attentive stance, the adults have an opportunity to put words to experience. The child gradually identifies and more fully expresses their inner life. They integrate the meaning given to the experience through the interwoven perspectives of self and other.

These are stories of experience extending the 'what happened' to 'what is the experience of what happened'. The child's experience is not judged or evaluated but accepted. This allows the experience to become integrated into the narrative the child holds about themselves and the world around them.

When witnessing their own story is too overwhelming for the child, the therapist and parent can use metaphorical stories to allow the child to witness their story at one remove. Children's books and therapeutic stories provide a treasure trove that parent and child can dive into. However, writing stories with and for the child can be even more powerful.

REFLECTION MOMENT

★ What story would you write for a child you are supporting?
★ What story would you write for yourself?

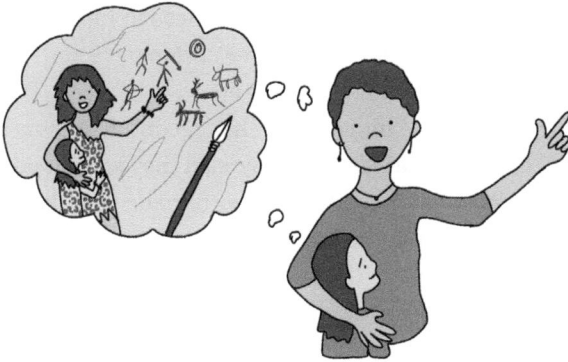

Humans are storytellers

IT

She had always known 'IT' was there waiting for her.

'IT' hovered on the edges of her consciousness as she went about the day.

'IT' haunted her as she tried to sleep. She felt its hard edges in her dreams.

'IT' called to her, taunted her, let her know it was what she deserved. Always 'IT' whispered: 'Not long now. It's coming. Not long.'

She wasn't exactly sure of the shape, depth or colour of 'IT'. It appeared to her as a void, a deep hole that she could fall into and never return. This hole waited for her, ready to swallow her up. She didn't know what lay beyond. She feared both nothing or something.

And so she carried on living her life, haunted by IT's presence.

She went to school, and the teachers complained at her lack of concentration, her fidgeting, her forgetfulness. How could she stay calm and focused when always she was aware of 'IT' just beyond her reach?

Her schoolmates kept their distance. Occasionally one of them would offer friendship but it rarely lasted. They complained she was weird, strange, different. They couldn't understand. How could they when they did not experience the fear she felt?

Her parents told her they loved her, but they loved the girl they saw, not the girl hidden inside. They didn't know her.

They hadn't been there at her birth when the social workers took her away; her birth mother already seeing the badness in her.

They weren't there when her first foster carers gave notice on her placement. They recognized that she was bad.

They were there when she moved from her second foster carers, but they were not told how bad she was. The judge said they were good enough to adopt her but even the judge didn't know that she was the one who was not good enough. She was the one that carried badness in her soul.

They took her to a therapist. They offered her strategies, tools, ways to manage the feelings that always felt too much. She tried, she really did, but the therapist didn't know that she couldn't use these things when 'IT' was so close and so big.

Her parents got frustrated with her. A little bit more of her curled up inside. She was waiting, just waiting for 'IT' to consume her.

And when she exploded, when the fear poured out of her in rage, despair and longing, they all became angry with her. And the voice got louder. 'Not long now. It's coming. Not long.' 'IT' was getting closer and closer.

She expected the new therapist to be the same as the last one. She braced herself for more lectures on things she could do. She rehearsed the feelings she'd be expected to recognize in her body. She practised the relaxation exercises that never seemed to keep 'IT' away.

But, this was different. The therapist didn't want to know about the feelings. They didn't tell her about what to do when the feelings got bigger. They chatted. They joked. They were interested in her. They paid attention to her. And she found herself revealing little bits of herself. Some of it she made up – how could she talk about herself when her self had been buried under fear for so long? The therapist looked at her, through her and saw the make believe. She braced herself. Now it would come. It didn't. She was accepted in her truth and in her fantasy.

A story was discovered between her and the therapist. A story about who she was and who she'd like to be. The therapist helped her to tell this story to her parents, who embraced her and told her they would always support her. She wanted to lean in. She wanted to believe. She longed to be embraced, loved and cared for. The longing grew but so did the fear. When would they discover the other parts of her, the parts that held the badness? When would they know she couldn't be who they wanted her to be? Not long now. IT's coming. Not long.

And then one day she couldn't bear it any longer. 'Come and take me,' she called. 'I don't know where I'll go when I fall, but waiting to find out is unbearable. I know I'm bad. So, take me now.' She picked up a pair of scissors and cut both arms. Anything to stop the pain while she waited for 'IT' to claim her at last.

Her parents found her. They bandaged her arms. She saw concern and disappointment in their eyes. She felt despair. 'Why do you taunt me so? Why do you say not long now but leave me here?' Her parents called the therapist.

The therapist welcomed her. She saw concern in their eyes. She looked for disappointment too. It wasn't there. The therapist gently and slowly explored what had happened. The kindness was her undoing. She told them about her fear. She told them about her badness and then she told them about 'IT'.

She waited, not sure what would happen now. The therapist smiled and told her they had heard her. They told this story of fear and badness back to her. They let her know that it made sense that she would feel this way given what had happened to her. They also let her know that there might be another story that they could find together.

She understood that they got it. This is how she felt, what she believed, and they didn't judge her for this. She felt herself relax, just a little. The therapist helped her to tell her story to her parents, finding words for her when she couldn't find them herself. Her parents embraced her. They told her they finally got it. They understood and loved her still. She felt herself relax a little bit more.

That night her parents came to her at bedtime. They told her they would stay with her as 'IT' got closer. They would be with her in her dreams. They would all visit 'IT' together.

They kept their promise. They all walked hand-in-hand, closer to 'IT'. They stood at the edge of the dark hole and looked in together. The voice was there, 'Not long now. It's coming. Not long.' Her parents talked back. 'Who are you?' they asked, and the voice replied, 'I'm the badness. I'm waiting here. I've waited a long time. Soon, I'll be all of her and we can fall together.'

And then her parents saw 'IT' for who it was. 'You're not the badness,' they said.

'You're the infant who was taken from her mother when she longed for her comfort.

You're the child who needed her foster carers to hold her when she shook with fear and then when she concealed that fear under anger.

You're the school child who feels the disappointment of her teachers and her school friends.

You're our child who needs our love but fears that we'll see you and go away.'

The voice rose up in fear and terror and courage.

'And now you see me, what will you do?' 'IT' asked.

'We'll take you in. We've abandoned you for far too long. Our abandonment has created this hole. You're our child too.'

And the child embraced 'IT', recognizing its fear and terror and courage. They were one. And the parents embraced their child in all her parts.

'You see me,' said the child. 'We see you,' said her parents, 'and we love you.'

The child awoke and knew the dark hole was no longer waiting for her. Her parents were there to welcome her. 'We see all of you,' they said, 'and you are enough.'

6

Slowing Down and Trusting the Process

If you have done any DDP training or reading you will have heard the words 'trust the process'. They are quite scary words. They ask us to move our agendas gently to the background, to sit without a plan and to follow where the conversation leads us.

Whether practitioner to parent or practitioner/parent to child, we trust that in this meeting together something good will happen.

> **REFLECTION MOMENT**
>
> ★ What does 'trust the process' mean to you?
> ★ What makes it hard for you to trust the process?
> ★ What helps you to stay with it?

DDP teaches us to trust the process. If we take the time to develop relationships and allow room for conversations within these relationships, then integration and healing will follow.

> 'It takes trust to slow down and be with the child where they need to be.'

It can be hard to trust this process. It takes an act of faith to believe that slowing down and 'being with' can lead to change. Whether we are therapists or parents, we feel the urge to make this change happen. We

THE DDP GUIDE TO HEALING CHILDHOOD TRAUMA

feel as if we should be doing something – giving advice, solving problems, offering strategies, persuading, lecturing.

And the referrers, the commissioners, they seek these answers too. 'What are you doing?' they ask. 'Why are you not fixing this?' They wonder, should they seek elsewhere? Maybe a different approach, a different model?

> **'Slowing down gets you to where you want to be more quickly.'**

There are no shortcuts. Rushing for change can leave us very stuck.

Deep, transformational change only comes in time and with the power of the relationship. When we allow ourselves to go more slowly, we find things can happen.

There may be strategies that can help and solutions to immediate problems that can work. These can make life more comfortable for the whole family. They do not heal the trauma.

REFLECTION MOMENT
Can you recall a time when you slowed down?

★ What helped you to do this? What was the result?
★ If others got frustrated with you, how did you help them to understand the importance of this?

Slowing down does mean taking a longer road. It means holding the belief that at the end of the road what is needed will be there. Rushing to the end may feel like a shortcut, but shortcuts can make long delays. (You may recognize this sentiment spoken by Gandalf, if like me you are a Tolkien fan!) The child needs to be heard and seen. Their sense of who they are and what they hold inside needs to be totally accepted.

Think about the beliefs that children impacted by relational traumas typically hold. Notice their beliefs that they are damaged, contaminated, bad, naughty, unloved and unwanted.

We understand the narrative the children hold about themselves. We know that this is what their experience has taught them. It makes sense to us that they feel this way, given what they have experienced.

Can we hold on to the hope that in listening deeply to this narrative we offer them new and different relational experiences which help them to discover new narratives?

Consider how these children anticipate that revealing their vulnerability will lead to their abandonment. They will not be loved or wanted. This is a lot of vulnerability we ask them to share with us. We lead them gently to this sharing in the belief that it will help them. No wonder we need to go slowly, when we are asking them to do something which is so scary.

Have you ever wondered how being vulnerable can lead someone to be stronger? How does revealing vulnerability within relationships that accept and hold empathy for them lead to a process of change?

Bruce Ecker and colleagues[1] believe that the answer to this question rests in a paradox. If you believe you are bad and that revealing this will

1   Ecker, B., Ticic, R. & Hulley, L. (2022) *Unlocking the Emotional Brain: Eliminate Symptoms at Their Roots Using Memory Reconsolidation*. New York: Routledge Mental Health Classic Editions.

lead to abandonment, but then you are helped to show these beliefs and are not abandoned, you are left holding two incompatible beliefs. This is the paradox that needs to be resolved.

From a story of shame and terror: 'I believe I'm bad. If you see enough of this badness, you will abandon me.'

We offer the child experience which leads to an incompatible second belief: 'I believe I'm bad. You see this vulnerability. You don't abandon me.'

The paradox of the incompatible beliefs needs to resolve, and a new narrative of hope and resilience develop: 'I believe bad things happened to me. This made me vulnerable. You don't abandon me. I'm courageous and strong.'

We cannot change a child's narrative for them. We can offer them experiences that help this narrative to change from the inside.

This is the process we need to trust.

TRAPPED IN A VORTEX

He swirls within a vortex. All around he feels the pressure on him. It is terror. It is shame. He's not good enough, never can be. He was given away, lost, forgotten.

Long ago he had belief. There would be warm hands. There would be kind eyes. Now he knows, there's just loathing, there's just disappointment.

Hands reach in to pull him out of the vortex. He rejects these hands as false promises. They will not be warm. They will not be kind. He rages. He hides. He resists. He feels as if he's a monster and will never be loved.

And then, not just hands reaching in, but hands joining him. They are in the vortex too. They see his terror and his shame. They understand his fear that he can never be good enough, that he's monstrous. They know he was given away and understand he fears their loathing, their disappointment.

He shouts. He rages. He hides. And still they stay. They offer warm hands. They show kind eyes. He turns away. He closes his eyes against them. Don't offer me hope and then take it away.

And still they stay.

It's hard, but they stay. Often, they wonder, can we do this? Are we strong enough? Are we good enough? It's taking such a long time. They risk falling into their own vortex. They need to be supported. They need warm hands to hold them, kind eyes to believe in them. Only then can they be strong enough to stay. And when it is too hard – when they leave the vortex, and their son – the support is there. Somehow this gives them strength. They find their way back in.

It's hard to resist when the warm hands and kind eyes keep returning. It's hard to believe in his monstrosity when it doesn't drive them away. He shouts less. He rages less. He hides less. They hold him, comfort him, gaze at him.

What do they see?

'We see you,' they say, 'our little boy.'

He is held by their arms. He looks into their eyes. He's not monstrous. He is a little boy.

Together they climb out of the vortex and make their way home.

7

Sitting with Vulnerability, However Uncomfortable

Together we have been exploring the concept of vulnerability. We have been focusing on helping another to be vulnerable. Now it is time to focus on us and what it is like to sit with a person who is being vulnerable.

REFLECTION MOMENT

★ How comfortable do you feel when with someone who is vulnerable?
★ Does this relate to your childhood experience?
★ Is witnessing vulnerability something you need to work at?

To improve my skill as a therapist, and as a parent, I've had to work at sitting with vulnerability. I have a strong need to make the other feel better as quickly as possible. This is probably because of my childhood attachment experience living with a depressed mother. Of course, all I succeed in doing is making myself feel better while leaving the other feeling unheard.

Is this something you recognize?

Maybe you had experience growing up with parents who were able to sit with your vulnerability. If so, do you think it is easier for you because of this?

As we've been exploring, there are no quick fixes. There are no short-cuts. We need to go on journeys with the children. We need to support them while they adapt to the world that they are now living in and recover from the world that they previously experienced.

Going on this journey requires a lot from us.

We must understand the child's vulnerability, while we also handle the behaviours that develop to hide this vulnerability from us and from themselves.

As we discover the vulnerability, we must sit with it. The child needs our love to be unconditional, 'I will love you no matter what.'

> **REFLECTION MOMENT**
> Reflect on the phrase: 'I will love you no matter what.'
>
> ★ What words or images capture the idea of unconditional love?

Trying to make the vulnerability go away risks it being hidden from us. Love becomes conditional. 'I will love you if...' This risks new behaviours arising to keep the vulnerability out of sight.

> **REFLECTION MOMENT**
> Reflect on the phrase: 'I will love you only if...'
>
> ★ What words or images capture the idea of conditional love?

Children need to know that their vulnerability is acceptable to us. They are safe to be vulnerable. We will not go away.

Sounds easy? Maybe not. As I write these words, the sun has just moved across the sky and is now shining into my eyes. Do I sit with this discomfort or pull the curtain to ease it? You can guess the answer. But what if the sun was the child's vulnerability? This question is not so easy to answer then. By pulling the curtain I am letting the child know that their vulnerability is not acceptable to me.

> 'When a child's vulnerability triggers our own vulnerability, we want to hide.'

What happens to you when a child makes you feel vulnerable? Do you doubt, sense failure, wonder if the child would be better off elsewhere? As a parent, I have experienced all of these.

Ghosts from our past may whisper to us: 'Remember, you are no good. Why did you think you could do this?'

All of this is uncomfortable, and therefore, as when the sun hurts our eyes, we may shield ourselves from it.

If we have grown up believing that showing vulnerability is a bad thing, we may fear what will happen if we stay with it. What will be unleashed if vulnerability is exposed. Many people have told me that they worry about opening 'Pandora's box'. They worry that if they open it, they won't be able to close it again. They won't be able to help the child.

If this is how you feel, remember that it is only by opening Pandora's box we find the hope inside.

> 'Vulnerability once seen loses its power. We find the strength to move forward.'

How do you feel about showing your own vulnerability or sitting with the vulnerability of someone else?

The idea does make me grimace; those ghosts from my past are still around! I do know that if I find people who hold acceptance and empathy for me, I will feel comforted. I can find compassion for myself and the courage to find acceptance for my child's vulnerability.

Meeting a child's vulnerability with acceptance and empathy is hard when all we want to do is make it go away. We want our child to be happy and safe and to develop well. It is hard when we cannot offer them these gifts. Instead, they need us to sit with them in their sadness, fear and struggles. Remember, they are living it every day. If we hide from it, we might feel better, but they will feel worse. With acceptance, we help the child to feel safe being vulnerable, to discover the support they have pushed away and to recover their own strength to move forward.

> 'The power of sitting with the uncomfortable for longer than is comfortable.'

PARENT AND CHILD

Child: Fear, hurt, terror, shame. They fill me up. These are unacceptable to you. I feel your disappointment. Happy, good, kind, compliant. I try to give you what you want. I fail. I'm overwhelmed. I hide. You try to find me and all I can show you is my rage.

Parent: I've taken you in. I've made you a home. I try to take away the fear, hurt, terror and shame. When you are happy, good, kind and compliant I think I'm succeeding. When you rage, I know I've failed.

Child: I know I'm not giving you what you want. I feel naughty, bad, not good enough. I don't know how to be any different.

Parent: I know I'm not giving you what you need. I feel helpless, hopeless, useless. I don't know what to do differently.

Child: Let me go. Send me away. I don't belong here. I don't want to stay.

Parent: Don't go, stay. We'll work this out. I cannot make you what you are not, but I can sit with you as you are. I know now this is what I need to do. I accept the whole of you. The fearful, hurting, terrified, shameful parts. I love them all. And when you don't believe in this, when you rage at me, I will love that part too. You're not naughty or bad. You're a child, and you are good enough. Let me demonstrate this to you.

8

Helping Children to Stop Fearing the Parents They Need Most

We are going to explore the way that the experience of relational traumas strips children of their primary source of safety, the loving hands of parents.

What was your home life like?

For those of us who grew up in safe and loving homes, it can be hard to imagine fearing our parents. Healthy parents offer their children the security of attachment relationships. The child grows up feeling safe and wanted. They experience trust in being parented. With trust a child believes in the good intentions of their parents and knows that they are loved no matter what. This is a truth that they carry even when the parents put limits on their behaviour.

For those of us who did not have this birthright, the fear is all too real.

Parents who have their own difficult histories of relationships, mental health struggles and/or current stresses associated with homelessness, poverty, drugs and alcohol may struggle to offer their children security. The child can be left with feelings of helplessness and a sense of not being good enough. This in turn can trigger fears of abandonment – fears that are confirmed if the child must leave the birth family because of concerns for their safety.

You can imagine how this can be a traumatizing experience for the child. Does it make sense to you that they can grow up fearing parents who they have experienced as frightening?

> 'When parents are more frightening than strangers, the child feels helpless and abandoned.'

The children I have worked with have shown me how strangers can feel much safer than parents. I suspect that this is one of the reasons for the so-called 'honeymoon period' which is sometimes observed when children move to a new family.

I remember one three-year-old adopted child who settled well for a six-month foster placement and for the first six months in her adoptive home. She then started to reject her adoptive mother. The poor mother thought she had done something wrong. I believe this child felt safe until this mother felt like a parent. Her experience of her birth mother, who had a severe psychosis, was very frightening.

I wonder if you have supported or parented a child who had a fear of being parented. Let's explore what this might feel like.

REFLECTION MOMENT

If you have had difficult experiences being parented, look after yourself and go as far with this reflection as feels okay.

I'm going to ask you something that I often ask in training. I want you to imagine something you fear, maybe spiders, snakes, the dark. Only imagine this as far as you are comfortable. I want you to be able to sleep tonight!

Imagine that you are in proximity with this thing that you fear. Notice how this feels in your body. Notice where you want to move to. Is there anyone that you want to turn to for help?

Stay with this experience as far as you can.

Now imagine being a child and replace the thing you fear with the image of a parent. As you imagine fearing the parent with all the same feelings in your body, consider what you now want to do to cope with this fear.

Join me in taking a breath and checking in with your body. Are you feeling settled?

Those of us who parent or support children impacted by developmental trauma witness how real a phobia of being parented can be.

Interventions for phobias often involve what we call graded exposure. We expose the phobic person to increasingly real experiences with the feared object, beginning with pictures, or experiences at one removed, until the person can tolerate a close-up experience without discomfort.

You will immediately notice that this is not possible for children frightened of being parented. Children cannot live alone; parents in one form or another must be in their lives. It is the equivalent of another intervention for phobias called flooding. The person is exposed to the most feared situation straight away and must tolerate it until their anxiety reduces. This intervention is rarely used now because of the level of distress it causes. It asks parent and child to manage something that is really hard.

'Innate trust in parents is blocked when being parented brings fear and pain.'

I want to bring in one more concept to help us understand this fear. You may have heard of the phrase: 'blocked trust'. Jon Baylin and Dan Hughes[1] coined this phrase to help us understand that while any child might move in and out of mistrust of their parents, developmentally traumatizing experiences of parents can actively block trust.

This is how Dan Hughes described blocked trust at a DDP conference in Birmingham, UK, in 2014: 'Blocked trust is when young children block the pain of rejection and the capacity to delight in order to survive in a world without comfort and joy.'

REFLECTION MOMENT

Reflect on a child who does not feel safe being parented.

★ How does this child keep themselves safe?

Now reflect on a child who is safe being parented.

★ What things does this child do that the first child can't?

Did you notice that the second child has experiences of being comforted and of playfulness with their parents that the first child doesn't?

We have been exploring what fear of parents is like. I expect you are wondering what we can do to help or maybe you are thinking about things that have helped a child you are supporting or parenting. I guess you agree with me that we can't just expose children to being parented and expect them to feel safe.

DDP approaches aim to restore parents as a source of safety for a child. This means supporting the current parents to offer safe attachment relationships even when these are being rejected. Parents hang in there while children test out the safety of the emotional connections on offer.

You may have experienced the resilience needed to do this while experiencing very rejecting and hurtful behaviours from the child. Support for these parents is essential, as we explore later in this book.

---

1   Baylin, J. & Hughes, D.A. (2016) *The Neurobiology of Attachment-Focused Therapy.* New York: W.W. Norton & Co.

Therapy for the child, involving the parents, can also create experiences with the parents that help children to overcome their fears.

> 'DDP approaches help the child to engage in emotional connection, and to feel less alone.'

THE FEAR OF A LITTLE GIRL

Nikole feels her tiny hand encompassed by the large hand of her aunt as they walk to school. She experiences no comfort in this small act of protection, only a fierce desire to run away. She has lived with her aunt for 18 months, moved there by the police when she was found roaming the streets as a three-year-old. After 18 months, and despite her aunt's best efforts, she feels no safer than she did at home with her birth parents, where there was little food and no protection.

As they draw closer to school, the buildings grow bigger and more imposing. Nikole looks for an opportunity to get away but her aunt knows her well. She holds on tight until she can hand her over to the teaching assistant who comes out to greet them.

Nikole is encouraged to play with the other children until the bell signalling the start of school rings. She only watches, standing at the edge of the playground, every nerve tingling at the imagined dangers that are all around her.

The assistant takes Nikole into the classroom a few minutes ahead of the other children. She settles Nikole into a chair near the front where the teacher can keep an eye on her. Nikole's neck aches as she constantly swivels around, checking who is coming into the room, who is walking past and who might be roaming the school grounds.

She notices a man in what looks like a uniform and tenses before she realizes it's not a policeman but the man who helps them to cross the road. Her aunt calls him a lollipop man because the sign he carries saying, 'Stop, Children Crossing' is in the shape of a lollipop. Nikole smiles for a moment but it's quickly gone. The teacher enters the room and Nikole is braced for the next threat.

Nikole is exhausted. She has engaged in few of the classroom activities and kept her distance from the other children. At breaktime, her teaching assistant takes her into a sensory room which relaxes her a little, but the noise and brightness of the classroom soon takes that away. Now it's nearly lunchtime and she knows her aunt will soon be picking her up.

Nikole does not want to go home.

Nikole does not want to stay in school.

Nikole wants the perceived safety of being out on the streets away from all these adults who seem so threatening.

One of the other children is feeling unwell. Nikole sees her chance as both adults are attending to the little boy. She quietly walks out of the classroom. A delivery is being brought into school and the front door is open and unattended. Nikole seizes the opportunity. She is out and crossing the school grounds.

Nikole roams around the periphery. A break in the hedge attracts her attention. She can just squeeze under the fence, her small frame allowing her to wriggle through the tiny gap.

Nikole relaxes as she wanders through the village. No one is about as she amuses herself banging a stick along the front gates of the houses. She notices she's hungry. The house with the blue door attracts her attention. Blue is her favourite colour. She walks up to it. Standing on tiptoes she can just reach the knocker.

The elderly man who comes to the door is astonished to find a small child on his doorstep. Nikole tells him she's hungry. He takes her indoors, telling her he'll find her something to eat.

Nikole reaches her small hand into the large one of the elderly man, and feels safe for the first time that day.

P.S. This story is based on a real event. The elderly man was safe. He made the child a sandwich and while she ate it he called the school. Child and aunt were reunited, and the school fence repaired.

9

Helping Children With the Impact of the Past on the Present

Do you remember in Chapter 7 I mentioned ghosts from our pasts? Let's return to this theme now, but from the child's perspective.

To understand this, it is helpful to reflect on how we are influenced by the experience of others.

> **REFLECTION MOMENT**
> Think about significant past relationships.
>
> ★ Do you recognize any lasting impact on how you see yourself or what you expect from others?

As we know, humans are a social species. Learning about ourselves and developing expectations about the world are embedded in the experience of others. This occurs because we have intersubjective (emotionally connected) experiences with those we are close to. We develop the meanings of our social-emotional world through these shared experiences. Our attachment relationships influence how we see ourselves and how we understand the world.

Our past relationships therefore have an important influence on us. Our sense of identity develops out of these shared emotional experiences. Our expectations are shaped by the shared understanding of the world and others.

Our past relationships give us a lens through which to view and understand the present.

I hope the relationships you reflected on were positive ones.

Healthy relationships provide us with integrated experiences of self and others. We develop coherent narratives of who we are and what we expect. These narratives help us to navigate the present unhindered by the past. Our past has helped us to become the person we are, able to move ahead independently.

Positive experience of attachment relationships provides us with the security to move forward confidently and to navigate tricky times with resilience.

You may have experienced less healthy relationships. Do you notice that these have a different influence on you?

> 'Current relationships viewed through the lens of past relationships take away the safety net of security.'

Traumatizing relationships offer an experience within which past and present become muddled. Our memories and perceptions lack the integration and coherence of those made within healthy relationships, and parts of us remain frozen in the past. When current experiences remind us of experiences from the past (sometimes called 'triggering'), these younger frozen parts take over and we act as if we are back there.

The lens through which we view and understand the present is now distorted by the events of the past.

REFLECTION MOMENT
Reflect on a child you know.

★ Think about the ways in which their current relationships take on the appearance of past relationships.

The children supported by DDP approaches typically lack a safety net of security. Their early relationships have provided experiences which have led them to view themselves as bad and the world as dangerous.

These past experiences mean that they struggle to navigate the ordinary tricky times that they inevitably experience in the present. They view their current relationships through the lens of their past relationships, their 'ghosts from the nursery',[1] and do not believe in the care and support being offered.

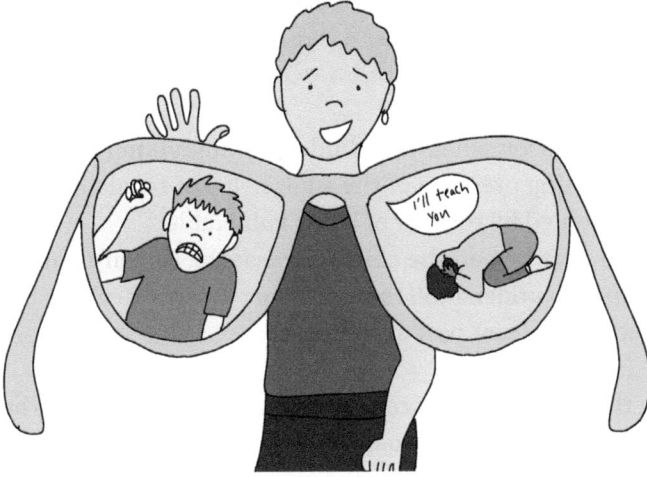

Can you see how the vulnerability which emerged in the past increases the child's vulnerability in the present?

Any resilience they develop is most likely to have emerged through self-reliance and not from the support of others. This resilience has shaky foundations. The children are reluctant to use the support others offer, fearing their past experiences. A range of controlling behaviours help them to hold on to a fragile security based on their own, often underdeveloped, ways of coping. These push away rather than draw in the support of others.

> 'Children who have been hurt within relationships view current relationships through the lens of this hurt.'

---

1   A concept introduced by Selma Fraiberg. See Karr-Morse, R. & Wiley, M.S. (1997) *Ghosts From the Nursery. Tracing the Roots of Violence*. New York: Atlantic Monthly Press.

I'm sure you can figure out how we use DDP approaches to help children to feel secure in their current attachment relationships, separated from their past relationships.

As with so many of the challenges we have discussed, this is done by offering them different relationship experiences.

There are two DDP principles which are important to help children separate past from present. Both are part of the affective-reflective dialogue we explored in Chapter 4, expanding into the storytelling discussed in Chapter 5.

- *Co-regulation* when the child is feeling vulnerable. The calm, supporting presence of the adult helps to regulate the emotion heightened by the fear of being vulnerable.
- *Co-creation* when the child's experience is confusing. They are helped to understand that their current experience makes sense because of their past experience.

Through the intertwining of co-regulation and co-creation, we help children to discover a coherent narrative that helps them to understand the past and to separate it from the present.

As the child discovers new meanings about their social-emotional world and about themselves, they experience their current relationships through a lens that looks to the present and not to the past. They have the safety net of security that healthy attachment relationships provide.

THEN AND NOW

Ten-year-old Nathan comes home from school. He excitedly hands a letter to his adoptive mother. His mother reads the letter with a sinking heart. It offers the children a chance to go on a school trip, but the cost is prohibitive.

As gently as possible she lets Nathan know that they can't afford this. She'll find a trip that they can go on together instead. She understands how disappointed he must feel.

Nathan explodes and for the next four hours he rages at her while throwing as many things as he can get his hands on.

For Nathan, the response from his mother has led to a collision between past and present. He is living in the now but experiencing the then.

Now (what is said)	Then (what is heard)
'I see you have a letter from school. You look excited. Let me see what it says.'	'What have you got now? You can cut out that excitement. Letters from school are never good news.'
'It's offering you a chance to go on a school trip. It's rather expensive.'	'I thought so. What idiots, giving you this. You don't deserve a school trip anyway.'
'I know you'll be disappointed, but I just don't have the money. We'll have to say no this time.'	'You think I've money to spend on you? What do you ever do for me? Now clear off to your room. I don't want to hear from you again tonight.'
'Let me find a trip you and I can go on instead. It won't be the same, but we can have some fun together.'	'I'm going to stop sending you to that school. It's more trouble than it's worth. You'd be more help to me here. You can take care of your sister.'
'I can see you're struggling. It's hard to hear me just now. I'm here. I'll help you with this struggle.'	'Stop your whining. You're worse than your sister. She doesn't give me the trouble you do.'
'I know it feels as if I don't love you when I say no. I'll always love you, even though it's hard for you to believe this right now.'	'They'll take you away if you don't quit. Shut up for goodness' sake.'
'You're my son. I love you just as much as your sister. We're a family.'	'You can go. We'll be better off without you.'

Nathan's rage eventually subsides. Mum is exhausted but knows she needs to stay with him. She needs him to feel that she's still here; to experience her presence so he can believe in her love for him. She cuddles him close and whispers to him that he's okay; she can help him. Nathan relaxes, too tired to fight any more. He seems to see her for the first time in hours. They sit amid the destruction of his rage until he is ready to talk.

Nathan's first concern is for his sister. He asks if she's okay. Mum reassures him that the neighbour is looking after her.

As they have talked about before, Mum helps Nathan to see that he slipped back into his past again. As Nathan is a sci-fi fan, they use the idea of a portal into his old home that Nathan sometimes walks through.

Nathan looks at his mum. 'I was so scared. You were so cross and mean. I thought you were going to send me away.'

His mum smiles at him. 'I know it seemed that way. Look at me. I'm here. You're here. I'll always come through the portal and bring you back to me.'

Nathan looks around and notices the devastation he has caused. He worries if he has broken anything. Mum reassures him that all the breakable things were out of his way. Nathan wants to start tidying up straight away but is persuaded to go to bed instead. 'It'll still be here tomorrow,' Mum says. 'We'll tidy it up together after breakfast.'

Later, with both children asleep, Mum gazes at them. They look so small and vulnerable. Mum knows that she's also feeling small and vulnerable tonight. These storms are so hard to manage. She can feel angry and helpless in the face of Nathan's rage. It's only the support of a good neighbour and the opportunity to talk things through with her support worker that help her get through it. She is able to hold on to some words that she and her worker had rehearsed together. The words provide her with an anchor as she experiences Nathan's storm. She hopes the next one will not last quite so long.

10

Helping Children Lower Their Shield Against Shame

How do you get on with understanding the concept of shame?

I found understanding shame and guilt to be tricky, with different people writing about them in different ways. It was therefore a relief to see how Dan Hughes described these. His separation of shame and guilt and the way that toxic shame can develop made sense to me. More importantly, I could see this in the behaviour of the children I was meeting and hearing about. For those of you who like to know the source for theories, Dan's ideas are based on the work of Tangney and Dearing.[1]

Dan talked about shame at a 2017 conference in the UK: 'When the infant or child asks the question "who am I?" – the core question of development – the answer that comes back is you are bad, shameful, an object for my use, disgusting, or nothing.'

It seems to me that experiencing shame is one of the most profoundly difficult experiences we can encounter. I recognize how much I want to hide when I have done something shameful. I really don't want others to know. The thought of being in this state all the time, as many of the children impacted by relational traumas are, fills me with compassion for them. I am also in awe when I see what these children can do and achieve when they are carrying this burden.

---

1   Tangney, J. & Dearing, R. (2002) *Shame and Guilt*. New York: Guilford Press.

REFLECTION MOMENT

★ What is it like when you have done or said something you are ashamed about? How do you handle the feelings that arise?

Reflect on what it is like when your whole identity is invaded by a sense of shame.

★ When are you ashamed for just being you?

Children who have been exposed to abuse, neglect and loss of family experience pervasive feelings of shame. When I experience shame, I recognize that I have done or said something which I wish I hadn't. I don't feel shame because I exist.

I wonder what your experiences of shame are like. For me, shame comes (not too often I hope!) but it also goes.

For children impacted by relational traumas, shame can be pervasive. This experience of shame is toxic to the developing sense of self.

'In your actions towards me, I know that I'm bad. I feel as if I shouldn't exist.'

Do you notice how much we humans like to find reasons for things? So, how do children make meaning out of traumatizing experiences?

Sometimes, the only reason that they can find for the meaning of their parents' abusive or indifferent behaviours is along the lines of: 'I'm bad, stupid, not good enough, unloveable.' Any other explanation would require finding fault with the parents.

An adult therapy client taught me how much a young child needs to believe in the goodness of their parents. In developing a sense of their own unloveability, they preserve an idealized image of the parent, who might one day see them as worthy of care.

By accepting that I had been an innocent infant with my own needs, I also had to accept that Mum couldn't meet these. It was at this time that I realized that it wasn't any unconditional mother that I wanted, I wanted my own mother. I wanted her to unconditionally love me. In accepting that it was not my fault that I had felt unloveable, I also had to accept that I could not make that better. No matter how 'good' I became, I could not make her what I needed her to be. This wasn't in my control. All the controlling behaviours I had found were now to no avail. This turned my world upside down.[2]

DDP approaches aim to regulate the child's shame. We therefore need an understanding of the experiences of the children.

So, let's have a refresher about the development of shame as I learned it from Dan.

Children develop a sense of their own loveability because of the countless moments of rupture they experience in their relationship with their parents and the subsequent repair of these ruptures. The parents' willingness to restore the attunement in the relationship signals to the child that they are loved no matter what. The shame they experience because of the rupture is regulated by the parents' repair, and the child experiences themselves as a good person even when things have gone wrong.

Notice that ruptures can arise because of actions of the child, actions of the parents, or moments of unavailability from the parents. Each of these ruptures carries within it the experience of devastation: 'This is the end. I'm no good. You will not love me.'

Shame threatens to engulf the child. Each act of repair by the parent reduces the experience of devastation and regulates the shame: 'It's okay. I am good. You love me.'

From these normal experiences of shame, the child learns that mistakes can be made, and that parents are sometimes absent, but this will be resolved.

When shame is regulated, children learn from their mistakes. They develop feelings of guilt instead of shame: 'I still know that I'm a good person. I recognize I made a mistake. I'll make amends.'

Guilt allows for feelings of remorse and children learn to carry out repairs of their own.

This is discipline at its best, an act of socialization: 'This is how I'm

---

2   Golding, K.S. & Jones, A. (2021) *A Tiny Spark of Hope*. London: Jessica Kingsley Publishers, p.116.

expected to behave in this home, in this community, in this culture. This is how I can make amends when I behave in ways you disapprove of.'

Regulated shame is protective and leads to children fitting into their communities and experiencing successful relationships.

So, what happens when the rupture/repair cycles are not present, when children are abandoned in the rupture?

When ruptures aren't repaired, there is no restoring of attunement in the relationship and shame isn't regulated. Instead of the development of feelings of guilt, remorse and the desire to make amends, the sense of shame grows and becomes part of the child's identity. This is what we mean by the expression toxic shame: 'I'm not a person who makes mistakes. I'm a person who is bad and you will always be disappointed in me.'

> 'Children who are bathed in toxic shame need a shield to survive.'

Living with shame and the expectation of disappointment from others is uncomfortable and potentially overwhelming. Defences are needed to keep the feelings of not being good enough out of awareness.

Children develop a shield against toxic shame.

REFLECTION MOMENT

★ What behaviours have you observed as part of someone's shield?

There are characteristic behaviours that a person displays when their shield is up. While these are the common behaviours we can observe, this is not a definitive list. Each child's shield might look different.

- Often, they *lie*. Even when caught in the act they claim: 'It wasn't me – I didn't do it.'
- They *minimize their actions*: 'It wasn't that big a deal.'

- They *blame others*: 'It's your fault. If you hadn't made me mad, I wouldn't have done it.'

Then there are the final behaviours, which are often the hardest to help:

- Total *rage* towards self, towards other, towards the world. The child communicates their distress, their sense of a world where everyone has it in for them and their own self-loathing.

- The children might need to *hide*. They take to their bed, and/or demonstrate self-harm and suicidal behaviours, all to escape the distress that they are feeling.

> **REFLECTION MOMENT**
> Think of a child who experiences toxic shame.
>
> ★ What behaviours are on their shield?
> ★ How can we help a child with their shield up?

DDP approaches need to understand the feelings of shame that the children hold.

The therapist works hard to see and connect with the feelings that lie beneath the shame. Therapist and parents then offer acceptance and empathy for these feelings. This helps to regulate the experience of shame.

Only when the child feels good enough in the eyes of their parents can they lower the shield.

In this way, DDP approaches seek to restore the child's sense of self as good and deserving of the kindness and care that parents are ready to offer.

TWO CHILDREN, TWO CATS AND A DIFFERENT RESPONSE

Kit and Cleo are both four years old. Nursery has finished for today and they have eaten lunch. They are now settling to play with some building bricks.

Kit	Cleo
Kit and their parent play together. They're busy constructing a castle with the bricks.	Cleo plays with the bricks while their parent sits nearby checking their phone.
Kit is enjoying playing. With the help of their parent they watch the castle build up as if by magic.	Cleo isn't sure what to do. They try balancing the bricks to form a tower and are frustrated when they topple over.
Freddie the cat strolls into the room. Kit is excited about the castle and wants to show it to the cat. Kit grabs Freddie by the tail and pulls him over towards the castle.	Tom the cat strolls into the room. Cleo notices him and abandons the bricks. Cleo decides the cat is a better playmate. Cleo pulls Tom by the tail and watches to see his reaction.
Kit's parent is cross. Kit has been told they have to be gentle with the cat. The parent is also worried that the cat could scratch Kit. They quickly move Freddie out of the way and tell Kit off.	Cleo's parent is cross. They just want Cleo to play quietly. They shout at Cleo. When Tom scratches Cleo, they angrily let Cleo know that it's their fault. That'll teach them.
Kit cries, shocked by the parent's anger and upset that they might have hurt Freddie.	Cleo cries. Their hand hurts from the scratch.
The parent comforts Kit. They tell them that it's okay. They're cross because Kit mustn't hurt animals. They want Kit to learn to be kind. The parent shows Kit how to be gentle with Freddie.	The parent shouts at Cleo. They tell Cleo that they'll give them something to cry about. Cleo stops crying and watches the parent leave the room.

Another day	
Kit is now five and is enjoying playing while their parent is busy. Kit knows the parent will be back soon.	Cleo is now five and wanders around looking for something to do. Cleo is not sure where the parent is and prefers to stay out of the way.
Freddie comes into the room. Kit goes over to him. He looks at Freddie's beautful thick tail and can't resist. Kit reaches out and pulls it, but then hesitates. This doesn't feel good. Kit doesn't want to hurt Freddie. They stroke Freddie to make him feel better. The parent comes in and smiles to see Kit and Freddie enjoying each other. They get some cat treats and enjoy feeding Freddie together.	Tom comes into the room. Cleo pounces on him. At last someone to play with. Cleo grabs Tom's tail and laughs as Tom hisses. Cleo dodges out of the way before Tom can scratch. The parent comes into the room. They yell at Cleo to leave the cat alone. Cleo angrily tells them that they didn't do anything. It was Tom's fault and anyway they're not hurt. The parent smacks Cleo for lying. Cleo rages, shouting that they'll kill Tom and the parent.

WHAT IS DDP?

WHAT IS DDP?

Part 2

PACE: THE THERAPEUTIC ATTITUDE

It's time to bring PACE centre stage in our explorations.

You may well know about PACE. It is the part of the DDP model that is most widely known. In this section, I want to dive deeper into an exploration of this attitude.

REFLECTION MOMENT

★ What does PACE mean to you?
★ Think of words, images, phrases and behaviours that sum up this way of being.

So here is my definition: PACE is a way of being that starts from a place of open engagement. When we are not defensive, we hold others in mind in a way that is similar to how they are experiencing the world. In contrast, when we are feeling defensive, we see others through the lens of our defences.

Open and engaged means that we:

- are *curious* about the other's experience without judgement and from a not-knowing stance
- genuinely wonder about their experience and seek to understand it more deeply
- hold *empathy* for this experience because we are fully *accepting* that this is their experience.

Playfulness

Acceptance

Curiosity

Empathy

Dan Hughes captured this therapeutic attitude in the acronym PACE.

The ACE of PACE has just been described. It helps us appreciate others more fully because we understand them better and feel with them more easily.

We then experience the joy of being in relationship with them and this allows a *playful* element to enter our interactions when this is appropriate.

ACE becomes PACE and we hold this as our way of being.

REFLECTION MOMENT

★ How easily do you embody the attitude of PACE?
★ Are there children this comes more easily with?
★ Are there actions you need to take that make it harder to maintain PACE?

Do you remember from Chapter 2 that when we interact with infants and very young children, this attitude comes relatively easily, despite sleepless nights and the frustrations that parenting can bring? We do this because we hold few expectations of these children. We are not preoccupied with how we want our child to be, and we more easily notice how they actually are. As children grow older, our responsibilities to guide, supervise, discipline and mentor them mean that PACE can slip into the background. It is not lost but it is no longer the only way our children need us to be.

Research has identified that the authoritative parent raises the best adjusted young people. Within the DDP model we see this as those parents holding the PACE attitude alongside the parental responsibilities needed to guide young people. Parents stay emotionally connected even at the hardest of parenting times. The young people know they are loved no matter what and more easily accept guidance and restrictions as a consequence.

REFLECTION MOMENT

★ Which of your childhood experiences have had most impact on the way you embody PACE?
★ Do elements of your upbringing make PACE easier or more difficult?

As we will explore in Part 5, we all come to PACE from our own cultural backgrounds and with varying experiences of playfulness, acceptance, curiosity and empathy during our upbringings. What comes easily to one parent is harder for another.

We also have the challenge of adjusting this way of being in a way that fits the cultural norms and expectations we live within.

The DDP practitioner has responsibility to understand the experience of the other, offering PACE in a way that is culturally acceptable and providing guidance that fits with the children and families' societal expectations.

This is a balancing act of finding the best fit between the needs of the child to develop trust, experience safety and overcome the impact of developmental trauma, and the needs of the parent to guide them into culturally acceptable ways of being in the world.

When children experience relational traumas, they often miss opportunities to experience secure attachment and emotional connections.

PACE offers the hope that the child can experience and be open to the influence of healthy relationships.

11

Please Anchor Me in the Safety of Your PACEfulness

I think of PACE as an anchor to hold me and others steady.

I hope you like metaphors, as I'm going to stay with this one. I also wonder what metaphors you would use.

> 'With PACE I never drift far from you. It is an anchor to hold us steady even in the turbulent times.'

Holding an attitude of PACE helps the DDP practitioner to stay open and engaged with the family. This supports the parents to stay open and engaged with their child.

When practitioners or parents become defensive, returning to this attitude can help them become available again. Like boats, PACE anchors us to safety again.

REFLECTION MOMENT

★ For each element of PACE, consider the quality that adds strength to the anchor.
★ Feel free to change the metaphor, if you have a different one in mind.

Children impacted by relational traumas bring challenges for those who are parenting them. Their mistrust, fear of emotional connection and need to control mean that they readily reject the offers of connection that PACE brings. They exist in defensive states and others then find it harder to stay open and engaged with them.

Holding an attitude of PACE helps parents and practitioners regulate and slow down in their responses. This anchor helps them to stay open and engaged, and to stop reacting and start thinking. This in turn guides their responses in a way which is helpful to the child.

REFLECTION MOMENT
Reflect on your own boat and anchor.

★ What supplies do you put in your boat? What strengthens your anchor?
★ What stormy waters might require additional preparation?

We all need support even though it can be hard to acknowledge this. Supportive others can be our port in the storm.

REFLECTION MOMENT

★ How do you recognize when you need to come into port for maintenance?
★ Who are the people you trust to provide this maintenance?

I expect that the people you most trust for support are those who hold an attitude of PACE for you. I believe that DDP practitioners who have a good understanding of PACE embedded into their practice can helpfully support others when needed.

Through the parenting support practitioners provide, parents are more able to hold on to PACE at the times it is most resisted and most needed by their children.

The practitioner helps the children to start to trust in the intentions of their parents, even when they are feeling confused and unsettled by the responses that they are experiencing from them.

'You hold me steady with your PACE. Your steadiness helps me stay steady for my child.'

The additional security and safety this brings provides a foundation from which further DDP approaches are provided in a way that promotes recovery and healing.

NIKITA NAVIGATES INTO CALMER WATERS

Nikita is experiencing turbulent waters and his anchor is drifting. As a DDP therapist he's been working with the Logan family for over a year, and the work is beginning to feel frayed.

After nine months of progress, the onset of adolescence coinciding with a change of school for Jackson, bereavements in the wider family and financial pressures are putting a strain on all of them. Nikita has increased his offer of support to the parents, although missed appointments means that this is not having the impact he hoped for. They are becoming increasingly frustrated and disappointed with the lack of progress and are demanding something different from him.

Jackson is still attending his therapy sessions, although with less empathy from his parents, the safety of these sessions is threatened.

Jackson is pushing Nikita hard, as if challenging Nikita to give up on him. He knows just what buttons to push, and his increasingly targeted and homophobic comments are becoming harder to manage.

Added to this, Nikita's relationship with his long-term partner is experiencing its own rocky waters. How do these kids know!

It's time for Nikita to bring his boat into port for some much-needed repairs.

Nikita books some additional supervision, giving himself permission to create space for some self-reflection. This is not easy, and Nikita launches into all the challenges that the family are facing, whether he is missing something, and how he might support them better.

His supervisor holds her hands up. 'Slow down, Nikita,' she says. 'Let's take a breath and think about you. I see this is impacting you hard.'

For the next half an hour, Nikita reflects on the challenges he's experiencing and how triggering these are. He admits that he's finding it hard to like Jackson and this is making it more difficult to remain open and engaged with him. He also worries that if he doesn't address his comments then Jackson won't learn and his homophobic views will become entrenched, extending beyond the therapy room. Nikita is torn between staying with acceptance and empathy, and providing some gentle challenge.

His supervisor empathizes with the difficulties in providing boundaries while maintaining therapy as a safe space. She expresses confidence that he will find the right balance. She is curious, though, about his growing feelings of dislike and wonders if they could explore this.

Nikita feels uncomfortable but knows this is important and he trusts his supervisor's non-judgement. He sits quietly for a moment thinking about Jackson. 'It's not the insults,' he muses. 'I've learned how to manage these over the years. It's something else.' He imagines himself back in the therapy room with Jackson and notices a sense of shame within him. His supervisor encourages him to stay with this. 'Notice and welcome this shame,' she suggests. 'See where this leads.' With this gentle support, Nikita closes his eyes and greets the shame with compassion. As he does so, a memory arises. He is Jackson's age and with his schoolmates. Nikita opens his eyes. 'I know,' he says. 'The insults Jackson uses are the same ones I used. It was before I came out. I was trying to protect myself by attacking others. I couldn't face discovering who I was. I carry a lot of hurt over those insults and the harm I caused. I was just a kid though. I didn't know how to deal with everything I was experiencing; it was a hard time. Jackson is a good lad. I don't want this to hurt him. He's struggling so much with feeling not good enough right now.' His supervisor smiles. 'I see you have your empathy back,' she says, 'for both of you.'

Nikita decides he will think some more about this with his partner. He grimaces as he recalls the hurtful things he said to him that morning. They need to get back on track and support each other as they have always done. He thanks his supervisor, noting that for now he has got what he needs.

They return to focusing on the family and the pressure Nikita is experiencing from Jackson's parents to 'fix' Jackson. He's feeling the burden of this.

As Nikita experiences the PACEful responses from his supervisor, he feels himself calming. It's always hard to see a family moving into a crisis of circumstances which threatens to derail the progress they've been making. Nikita can now reflect on what the family need and why he is feeling challenged.

Nikita has a good relationship with Jackson's parents. He can trust them to guide Jackson in his behaviour. They can talk about this when they next meet. What Jackson needs from Nikita is understanding and empathy for the difficult emotions he's experiencing underneath this behaviour. He's forgotten to trust the process; to anchor himself in PACE and to extend this into the DDP sessions; to offer a calm port to help them all navigate the storm they're finding themselves in.

Nikita arranges a family session. He takes a breath as they enter the room. The attitude of PACE at the centre of his work is strong again and the family feel listened to.

When Jackson begins with the insults, Nikita lets him know that these are hurtful, and then notices the worries Jackson is experiencing and how hard things are. Jackson softens a little, and his parents respond with empathy instead of chastizing him as in recent sessions.

When the parents worry about the lack of progress, Nikita is empathic and curious. He wonders how they're making sense of this. He understands their worries that he might be missing something, while noticing the impact of multiple life events occurring at the same time.

They all pause, take a breath and notice how much the worries are piling up. Jackson tearfully acknowledges the sadness he is feeling at the loss of a beloved grandfather and his worries about where the current financial problems might lead. His parents realize that, preoccupied by their own sense of loss and worry, they've not been aware of the extent this is impacting on Jackson.

Nikita notices the family coming together. They still have turbulent waters to navigate, but PACE is a strong anchor again. It keeps them all steady while they journey into calmer waters.

12

I Need Your PACEful Presence More Than Techniques

Have you, like me, heard people talk about PACE as if it is a technique? If behaviours don't change, they tell us that PACE is not working. They have lost sight of PACE as a way of being to build security.

REFLECTION MOMENT

★ What words or images capture your experience of PACE as a way of being?
★ How can you demonstrate this way of being as different from technique?

We all want children's challenging behaviours to change, and there is always space for discipline. However, real behaviour change only emerges when children have a growing sense of safety and security. In trusting us, they more easily accept our behavioural guidance.

So, how can we help others to understand what PACE is and is not?

Here are my thoughts:

- If PACE is used as a technique to change behaviour, acceptance of what the child is feeling is reduced. Without acceptance, we are not being PACEful.
- Children react to pressures to change with

shame, as they experience not being good enough. This can lead to resistance, strengthening the behaviour instead of reducing it.
- When we sit alongside children, understanding and accepting their experience, the children get a sense of being good enough. They are then more open to guidance about their behaviour.

This might help people to understand PACE more deeply. Can you guess what their next question is?

How can we guide children into more acceptable behaviours?

This is a fair question. We cannot tolerate unacceptable behaviour. Children need boundaries and discipline to develop the social behaviours that help them to fit in, succeed and have good relationships.

REFLECTION MOMENT

★ How can behavioural guidance be introduced to children in a way that is non-shaming?

The important point to convey is that we can't make a child change their behaviour. The stubbornness of mules comes into my mind as I write this. The more we try to urge them on, the more they dig their hooves in!

However, we can change our response to the child. As we change our response, behaviour change can happen. Instead of tugging at the mule, we respond to it in ways that make it want to follow us.

REFLECTION MOMENT

★ What can parents offer that leads to children wanting to change their behaviour?

Here are my top three. You might recognize the influence of PACE on these!

- *Understanding:* Showing the child you get why they have behaved as they have.

- *Warmth and nurture:* Empathy for the struggles they are having.
- *Acceptance:* Helping the child to know that they are acceptable to their parents even when their behaviour is disapproved of.

I have also known parents who are brilliant at being *playful* at just the right moment, without detracting from the message that the behaviour is unacceptable. This is a skill I would love to have!

> 'I cannot change your behaviour, but I can change my response to it.'

Okay so far, but you probably know what the next question is.

That is all very well but what do I do when the children reject all this lovely parenting you want me to offer?

Again, a good question. Developmental trauma has entered the scene.

When the child has little trust in being parented, it is hard for the parent to convey their love for the child, alongside the discipline needed to help them succeed. If the child doesn't trust the parent's good intentions, ordinary discipline reinforces for the child beliefs that they are unloveable and will be abandoned.

This can take a huge toll on the parent, leaving them with a sense of failure and uncertainty about what to do next.

How easy it is for parent and child to turn away from each other as they experience the disappointment that failure can bring. Each maintains the behaviours that are not helping.

The child continues to be challenging.

The parent increases their discipline.

At this point in the conversation, we might be feeling our own sense of failure. We are not finding an answer to 'fix' the parent's problem.

Do you remember: 'trust the process'. This is one of those moments.

It is going to take time for the parent to help the child trust them. Practitioners need to stay emotionally connected to the parent so that they stay emotionally connected to the child, even during times when discipline is needed.

This connection with discipline helps the child to trust in the parent's good intentions and to believe that they are unconditionally loved. Over time, increased security can lead to change and healing.

> 'PACE is a way of being that helps us to be emotionally connected to each other.'

PACE: A WAY OF BEING FOR ALL AGES
A parent gazes at their infant

Emotional connection comes easily to them as they hold this tiny, defenceless child. They are instinctively curious about what this infant is experiencing. Are they hungry, in discomfort, tired, bored?

They test out their guesses. The child responds to their playfulness. Hunger takes over; this too is accepted.

Empathy feels natural for a child who is dependent on them to meet their needs. PACE is an easy way to be with their infant. They hold the knowledge in their bodies, embedded by their own healthy experiences of being parented.

The infant grows into a toddler

The parent needs to put boundaries in place. The child finds their voice and protests at restrictions to their developing autonomy.

The parent provides emotional connection, enjoying these moments of togetherness and soothing their distressed child when these connections are lost.

PACE remains central within their parenting.

The child goes to school

This is a big transition for child and parent as the child's world, independent from their parent, grows larger.

The parent finds ways to help the child feel emotionally connected while they are apart.

Their increasingly verbal communications continue to show interest in the child's emotional world. The playful, accepting, curious empathic relationship that the parent offers maintains their connection, shows interest in the child, and continues to soothe moments of worry and distress.

Transitions follow transitions as child grows into adolescence

Growing independence, increasingly important friendships and an instinct to move out from the family might seem to make emotional connection with parents less important.

The youngster still needs the safe base of home to return to. They need their parents' continuing interest and guidance, even when they appear to shrug this off. They need warm arms and a kind heart to embrace them when life feels difficult.

'Laugh with me, know me, understand me, do not judge me, guide me, pick me up when I falter.' This is the backdrop adolescents need as they mature and discover who they are.

And the parents who go on these parenting journeys

They too need support. Others holding PACE for them helps them to stay steady in their PACEfulness even at the toughest times. Relationships, emotional connections, and opportunities to laugh and cry together are what get us all through the ups and the downs.

PACE truly is a way of being for all ages.

13

Enjoy Me; Play With Me

In this chapter, we explore the P of PACE.

The first element in the acronym, playfulness, is the element that comes and goes most. I expect you can think of times when you have enjoyed another's good natured playfulness and times when this has not been appropriate.

I wonder if you are someone who relishes being playful. Do being and responding to playfulness come easily?

Or are you, like me, someone who can feel uncomfortable in playfulness?

REFLECTION MOMENT

Reflect on times you have been invited to play.

★ What helped you to respond and what stopped you responding to these invitations?

Temperament (shy or outgoing) and our own upbringing (how much playfulness we experienced growing up) both have a role in how natural playfulness feels.

We all have the capacity to enjoy being in relationships. This brings a lightness to our interactions that can also be described as playful. Full-on or quietly, playful interactions are important to relationships.

'The best play conveys interest in the child and joy in the relationship.'

Playfulness signals to the child that they are okay and that the parent is interested in them.

What do you think destroys playfulness more than anything else? I imagine us all as one saying: 'trauma'.

REFLECTION MOMENT
Think about a time when you have invited a child to play.

★ What helped them to respond and what stopped them responding to your invitation?

Any trauma will impact on playfulness. The experience of relational traumas is particularly burdensome for children. They carry these burdens in their nervous systems.

In response, the nervous system develops finely tuned defensive ways of responding to threats that might be real or imagined. The children live in states of fight, flight, freeze and shutdown. They adopt controlling strategies rather than connect with others. They struggle to rest, relax, and to sleep. All their energy goes into surviving the threats that their over-sensitive nervous systems perceive.

Stephen Porges[1] helps us to understand how these defensive states block social engagement. Without this, the children struggle to explore, to be curious, to enjoy novelty and to play.

1   Porges, S.W. & Porges, S. (2023) *Our Polyvagal World*. New York: W.W. Norton & Co.

To help their children recover playfulness, parents need to soothe their children's hypervigilant nervous systems. They offer the children an environment that constantly signals that they are safe. They convey the joy that they feel in their relationship with the child.

The past recedes as the present feels less threatening and the door to play opens.

Can you think about any other positives of play?

I have one more to share with you, and it is to do with intimacy and affection.

How many children do you know who struggle with affection? They might reject it. They might cling to it without ever feeling soothed. They do not relax in the comfort being offered. Imagine how play can be a gentle way into intimacy. The child might tolerate some affection in brief moments of playfulness, which demands less of them.

REFLECTION MOMENT

Reflect on different ways of being playful.

★ Can you think of any cautions about bringing playfulness into parenting?

Here are a couple of cautions I have in mind.

Play can be sneaky.

Sometimes we use it in a way that gives a child a message. Disapproval, veiled in a tone of fun; sarcasm, which disguises a message as a form of play.

These are communications that are confusing to the child. The parent seems interested in them and their relationship: I am playful. At the same time, there is a contradictory message that says: I am disapproving. I want you to behave differently.

These messages carry threat and signal danger to the nervous system. The child moves into a defensive state again.

'Play is given with a clear message: I'm enjoying my relationship with you.'

Play can be competitive.

This is not necessarily a bad thing. Secure children thrive with appropriate competition. They build skills, resilience, and an ability to cooperate and to manage conflict.

Insecure, traumatized children may not be ready for such competition. They do not feel good enough, and this can drive a need to be the best, to win, to be first. This increases conflict and reduces the ability to cooperate.

Competitive play needs to be introduced slowly and cautiously.

When I was at university, I had a group of friends who decided to play 'the ant's game'. At some point in the day, one of the group would call 'ants' and everyone in the group had to immediately lie on their back and kick their arms and feet in the air. They thought that this was hilarious. I hated this game. I found it embarrassing and exposing. I could not join in and felt alienated from the group.

Why am I sharing this memory with you? I think it arose while I was writing this chapter because it shows how individual play is, and how hard it can be when we feel different. If we are interested in the other person, we learn how they like to play. That is how we demonstrate that we enjoy the relationship. That is the P of PACE.

THE PATHWAY TO PLAY AND A HOPEFUL FUTURE

Protect me.
I come to you full of fear.
Let me know I am safe.

Calm me.
I see danger everywhere.
Show me how to relax.

Play with me.
I don't know how to have fun.
Show me in your enjoyment of me.
Now I can look to the future with hope.

14

Accept Every Part of Me

We are going to continue to explore the PACE elements, in the order they appear in the acronym. Of course, PACE is not linear. We weave in, out, between and round the elements, as PACE becomes a whole way of being.

So, let's focus on acceptance, the A of PACE.

REFLECTION MOMENT

Reflect on what acceptance means to you.

★ Is there an image or a colour, maybe a sound, a song, a smell, that represents acceptance to you?

How long have you been aware of the importance of acceptance within relationships?

It seems to me that the principle of acceptance as part of therapy has been around for a long time, but the value of acceptance in parenting relationships is less understood.

Do you agree with me that helping others understand acceptance is the hardest part of PACE?

To understand acceptance, we need to understand that there is an inner world where we hold our experience – what we think, feel, believe, and wonder about. This is a private space which others can't see, and so we communicate this inner experience through language and behaviour.

This inner world can be validated. Another person understands and accepts that this is the other's experience.

> 'Your thoughts and feelings are neither right nor wrong;
> they just are. My acceptance of this helps you to trust in your
> acceptability to me.'

It can also be invalidated. The other person may understand but does not accept it. They want the other person to think and feel differently.
Consider the difference between:

- 'I hear you when you tell me that you hate your brother. I understand that this is how you are feeling right now, especially as he ate the last cake! I'm sad you feel that you hate your brother and I hope you won't always feel this way.'

And:

- 'I hear you when you tell me you hate your brother. You don't hate him, you love him. He ate the last cake today and you'll get the last one another day.'

Can you see how, in the first example, the parent recognized how the child was feeling, and it was accepted and made sense of?

In the second example, the parent did not make sense of it; instead their child was told that they were wrong in what they were feeling.

REFLECTION MOMENT
Reflect on an experience when you felt invalidated.

★ How did it make you feel about yourself and the other person?

When a person is invalidated, the reality of what they are experiencing is being judged. In the example, the feeling of hatred was dismissed as the parent expressed that it was unacceptable to feel hatred towards the brother.

Invalidation feels psychologically unsafe because the person feels unsafe in the relationship.

Invalidation expresses disappointment.

Have you noticed how much children struggle when they experience a parent as disappointed in them?

> 'When you can't accept my inner experience, I hurt with the disappointment I bring to you.'

When this experience is extensive, it can lead to difficulties in understanding or expressing inner experience and is often at the root of mental health difficulties, linked to the experience of shame and the development of poor self-worth.

Acceptance of internal experience is validating because the other person feels understood and experiences this understanding without judgement; thoughts and feelings cannot be right or wrong, because they just are. This creates psychological safety and feels supportive and caring. It regulates feelings of shame and leads to the development of good self-worth.

Acceptance is a complicated element within PACE and can be misunderstood.

What have you found that people most worry about when asked to increase their acceptance?

I have found that people worry that PACE makes parenting 'soft' and without discipline. This is because they haven't understood the difference between accepting the experience of the child and tolerating the behaviour and language the child uses to express this inner world.

A child can struggle to express what they feel and think, especially when this experience is overwhelming. They may use language and behaviour that is not acceptable. As we mature, we find ways to express our experience without harming the relationship.

Parents have an important task in helping their children to develop this maturity so that children can navigate areas of conflict and learn to cooperate with others. For this reason, while inner experience is accepted, language and behaviour may not be tolerated.

Healthy parenting helps children to learn when their behaviour is not acceptable. It guides them into different ways of expressing their inner experience, while still validating them for this experience.

So far, so good, but again bringing developmental trauma into this adds another layer of complication. For these children, they often don't see the difference between their behaviour and themselves. Behaviour and identity get mixed up.

You will have heard the common phrase parents say to children: 'I love you, but I don't like your behaviour.' How confusing this must be when you do not experience a difference.

REFLECTION MOMENT

★ What have you noticed in children when their identity is wrapped up with their behaviour?
★ How does this confusion get expressed?

Can you see any other layers of complication?

The one I am mindful of is the impact on the parent of their child's experience of relational traumas.

There are some things that are hard for a parent to accept. For example, it is hurtful that their children are still distressed, fearful of them and lacking in trust when they have been working so hard to lessen these. The parents experience disappointment at their perceived failure.

The children notice this as a sign that they are not good enough, reinforcing the distress, fear and lack of trust.

The parent needs support and acceptance for their feelings of failure and then they can hold understanding and empathy for their child's experience. With this acceptance the child builds trust. Now they can allow the parent to gently guide them into new ways of being, feeling their acceptance when these become too hard again.

EXPRESSING ACCEPTANCE

Here are my thoughts on how we express acceptance. See if this sparks some thoughts of your own.

To express acceptance, the parent needs to understand what the other's internal experience is. Their accepting response conveys this understanding without judgement. This does not mean that they agree with the communication.

A child expresses that they are useless at painting while we admire what they are achieving.

Acceptance does not convey: 'Yes, I agree you are useless.' Instead, it conveys: 'I understand that you feel useless.' The child is understood.

The parent may then express their own experience: 'I feel sad that you don't like your paintings. I hope that one day you see your paintings as I do.'

A word about 'but'

'But' is a tricky little word. It was only when this was pointed out to me that I realized how often I use it! 'But' joins two thoughts together and sometimes this sends a hidden message: 'I hear that you hate your mother, but she is your mother and is doing her best.'

Imagine receiving this message. Notice how the second half of the sentence minimizes what you are communicating in the first half. Can you see that it suggests a judgement, 'you shouldn't hate your mother' and is therefore invalidating of the child's experience?

Did you notice my use of 'but' in one of my examples earlier? If not, you might like to look back and consider what 'but' does in the sentence. (Clue: it's just before the second reflection moment.)

Here are some examples of conveying acceptance:

- 'If that's what it feels like, I see how hard that would be.'

- 'I can understand why...'
- 'That makes sense to me. It's hard when...'
- 'That must have been tough for you. No wonder you feel...'
- 'Of course, you wouldn't want to talk about it if...'

MY MOTHER DOES NOT LOVE ME

Telise has had a hard life. Her birth mother emotionally neglected and abused her from birth. She surrounded Telise with chaos, and a lack of protection from all the people who came in and out of their flat, many of them intoxicated by drugs and alcohol. From an early age, Telise gave up trying to elicit a response from her mother. She sought sanctuary with a kind neighbour who called the authorities. Telise is now living safely in foster care.

The loss of Telise appears to remind her mother that she has a daughter. She demands the contact with her that she's entitled to. As Telise grows older she finds these contacts increasingly difficult. Her mother shows little interest in her. All she wants to do is tell Telise about all the troubles she's having. She encourages Telise to be difficult for her foster carer and social worker. Telise notices that her birthday is never remembered.

Telise plucks up her courage to talk to her foster carer. She tells him that she hates these contact visits, her mother doesn't love her, and she wants to stop seeing her altogether. Her foster carer listens with a frown on his face. He's unsure that the visits can be stopped. He tells Telise that her mother does love her really. She is her mother after all. Nevertheless, he offers to talk with the social worker.

The social worker visits. He listens carefully while his heart sinks. Telise's mother can be difficult. He doesn't fancy listening to one of her tirades if the visits stop. He reminds Telise that she is her mother, and she has asked for these visits. She does love Telise really but her life's been difficult, and it's hard for her to organize things.

Telise, usually a quiet, reserved child, explodes with anger. 'You're not listening to me. I hate seeing her. She has absolutely no interest in me. She only asks for the visits to make a point to you.'

They ask Telise to calm down and they'll think what to do. Maybe they can find a way to make the visits better for her.

Telise shouts, 'Don't you get it. She doesn't love me, and I don't love her.' She looks at her foster carer's face. 'And now you think I'm a monster.' In tears, she runs out of the room.

The social worker and foster carer talk together. They wonder about a mother's love for their child, and reflect on the experiences that brought Telise into care. They start to feel uncomfortable as they realize they weren't listening to Telise. Her experience is that her mother doesn't love her and she needs to be heard.

They call Telise down and apologize.

'We haven't been listening properly. You're telling us that your mother doesn't love you. Of course it feels this way when she doesn't show any interest in you and never remembers your birthday. We don't know why your mother behaves this way, and we can see you feel no love from her. We don't see you as a monster. How can you love someone when you can't feel love from them? We want you to know that we're hearing you.'

'At last,' says Telise. 'Now can I stop seeing her?'

The social worker promises to explore this. It might take a while and it might need to go to the courts to decide. He asks Telise to be patient, and he will keep listening to her.

15

I Need Your Curiosity

And so, we reach curiosity. I wonder what the 'C' in PACE means to you.

REFLECTION MOMENT

★ Do you have an image, colour, sound, song or smell that brings curiosity to mind?

Within PACE, curiosity and empathy inform each other. Together they guide us to acceptance of the internal world of ourselves and others.

And this brings us back to stories.

We all have stories, narratives we hold about ourselves, others and the world. These stories are about our current, past and expected future experiences.

'Our internal world creates stories. We discover these stories in our thoughts and feelings.'

Curiosity makes us explorers searching for these stories. We start from a stance of not knowing so that we truly discover without assumptions.

If we are not curious, we lack understanding. Our actions can only be directed by the assumptions we hold. These assumptions lead to rapid judgements, and we react rather than reflect. In reactivity, relationships are weakened.

REFLECTION MOMENT

Reflect on an experience where another person held assumptions about you.

★ What was this experience like?

On the other hand, our relationships strengthen when they are bathed in curiosity. We act on our understanding, and these actions are thoughtful and considered.

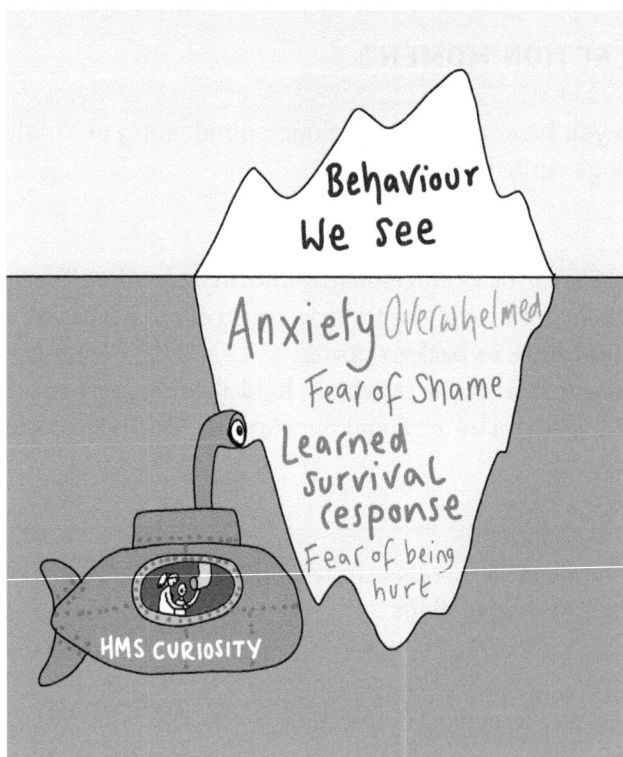

EXPRESSING CURIOSITY

How do you express curiosity?

I see curiosity as a genuine seeking to understand another by noticing, wondering and discussing their experience.

> **'Curiosity is the art of not knowing but discovering together.'**

We do this on their behalf; we wonder but without expectation that they know or that they can tell us their experience.

We also do this with them, if they can put their experience into words and are willing to join us in this act of discovery.

I believe that curiosity should not be rushed, hard as this is in modern times. Discovery takes time and stories build slowly. As you discover, new understanding is weaved into the narrative. This understanding has room for empathy, and empathy deepens the story.

Here are some examples of conveying curiosity:

- 'I'm wondering how that felt/what you thought, when...?'
- 'If I were you, I would be wondering...'
- 'What are the hardest things about...?'
- 'Help me to understand when...'
- 'How do you make sense of...?'

WHAT IS INSIDE THE BOX?

The box appears quite slowly. It wasn't there when the child arrived, or perhaps it was but was hidden from view. Over the months, they become more aware of it. It takes shape, a plain wooden box which goes with her everywhere. They also notice it growing. The longer she lives with them, the bigger the box.

This worries the parents, who have a sense that they are getting something wrong. They are failing as parents. They want to get rid of the box. They feel it weighing them down, weighing their child down. However, when they speak to the child, she denies it exists. Does she truly not see it or is she pretending it isn't there?

Teachers complain about the box. It shouldn't be in school. It is stopping the child learning.

Friends fall out with the child. They can't play properly because of the box. After a while they leave her alone.

And the box continues to grow.

The parents talk to their child. They tell her the box must go. They try to open the box, but all their tools are useless. They try taking the box away, but the next day it is back again. They even try destroying the box, but it just grows bigger.

And the child continues to deny it exists.

The parents talk to each other. They notice how much the box is affecting the family. No one is happy. How can they get rid of it?

The parents talk to the therapist. The therapist wonders about the box. What do they think it is? What do they think is inside? The parents don't know. They've been so busy trying to get rid of it they've never stopped to wonder.

'Start wondering,' says the therapist. 'I think it needs to be understood.'

Wondering is hard. The box gives so little away. They do notice patterns. Certain challenging behaviours of the child seem to make it grow, while other more cooperative behaviours make it smaller. When the child pulls away from them it seems to be heavier, but when the child is close to them, perhaps it gets a little lighter.

Hopefully, they encourage the child to cooperate. They also try to pull her closer. She resists both and the box weighs her down even more.

They remember what the therapist said and return to wondering.

They wonder out loud, and the child listens.

They make guesses, and the child comes a little closer. They ask the child what her guesses are. She shrugs. She doesn't know.

They ask the child if they can make guesses for her, and she says yes. And so, they guess. With each guess the child lets them know with a thumbs up or down if it feels right. Occasionally, the child even makes a little guess of her own.

The box grows smaller. It weighs less. It's just an ordinary brown box.

And then it opens. The parents explore its contents – everything their child feels and thinks but cannot tell them. The box tells them their child's story.

The parents hold their child close. She doesn't resist this time. They tell her the story that the box has held for her. It's a story of loss and longing and not feeling good enough.

As the child listens, she relaxes, and the story changes a little. As well as loss and longing and not feeling good enough, she feels the start of finding and belonging, and maybe being good enough after all.

The box sighs and fades. It isn't needed any more.

16

Feel With Me and Calm My Pain

Empathy is one of those words that is used a lot and confused a lot.

In this chapter, we explore what empathy, sympathy and compassion are, alongside how they influence our attitude of PACE.

I must admit when reading what various experts say about these terms, I find this confusing. Here is the sense I have made of it, but please do find your own way through this maze of terms as well:

- We have sympathy because we understand someone's experience, but we do this without imagining what it is like 'sitting in their shoes'.
- Compassion, like sympathy, is a more cognitive process of knowing but with more intention to know what it feels like from the other's position.
- In empathy, we offer our understanding to the other person by feeling with them.

> 'When you feel my empathy, you know that I understand and am feeling with you.'

We are back to hearts and minds again.

Compassion takes us further than sympathy as we want to use our mind to understand the other's story more deeply. Empathy expresses this story from our heart.

As always, we need both heart and mind. In knowing, we deepen our feeling towards someone. As we feel with them, we understand more deeply.

Does this make sense? I hope so.

Of these three terms, I think Dan Hughes chose empathy for PACE because he saw the importance of intersubjective experiences, feeling with someone.

It is through empathy that we make emotional connections and build healthy relationships. We show empathy to help the other person feel understood and emotionally connected to us.

REFLECTION MOMENT

Reflect on what empathy means to you.

★ Do you have an image, colour, sound, song or smell that brings empathy to mind?

Do you think empathy is one of those things that is easier to 'know' than to explain?

This is because we develop empathy from within relationships. If we experience empathy, we can feel it.

And for children impacted by relational traumas?

REFLECTION MOMENT

Think about empathy in relation to children you have known and their early experience.

★ Do you recognize children who are empathic but don't know what to do with this or who seem to have no empathy at all?

★ How do you think the experience of PACE can help these children?

You've guessed it, they struggle more with empathy because of their early childhood experience. PACE provides them with experiences of being understood and felt. With these experiences, their empathy develops.

'The empathy of PACE wakes up the empathy of the relationally traumatized child.'

EXPRESSING EMPATHY

I think we have all experienced children who have strongly reacted to experiencing empathy from others.

One reason for this is that empathy evokes vulnerability. A child who does not feel safe in the relationship does not want to feel vulnerable. The adult needs to tread lightly, muting their empathy to an acceptable level and only gradually increasing this as the child develops trust. By turning the dial down, or being more indirect, the caregiver helps the child to build their tolerance for empathy alongside an increasing sense of trust and feelings of safety.

Another reason is that empathy needs to be genuine. If an adult tries to use empathy as a technique, it is experienced as false and possibly patronizing. Authentic empathy emerges from understanding the other, especially as you witness areas of vulnerability.

Here are some examples of conveying empathy:
- 'You've had so many hard times when…'
- 'I see why you think… These are such uncomfortable thoughts to have.'
- 'I'm sitting here feeling so sad because…'
- 'That sounds like a big worry when…'
- 'Oh, it sounds like…was really tough.'

HOW EMPATHY CALMS THE VOLCANOS

He cannot remember a time when he did not carry the volcano within him. It is always there, sometimes quiet, sometimes active, and always ready to erupt. Big things set it off; of course they do.

- Fears that his uncle will not come back from his weekend away.
- Worries that his best friend will shun him again when he is with his other mates.
- Racist abuse on the bus as he travels to and from school.

The volcano ignites, and he yells at his uncle, fights his best friend, and hurls abuse at everyone on the bus, including the bus driver, until he is ordered to get off. He is always in trouble. They see the volcano, but not the scared child within.

Little things also set it off, although he doesn't know why.
- Not being first for breakfast.
- Not winning when they play games.
- Not being allowed to sit in the front of the car.

He knows that none of these things really matter, and yet the volcano stirs all the same. His uncle reasons with him, and he knows he is being unreasonable. The volcano erupts. He shouts, throws things, and he even hit his uncle once. He sees the disappointment in his uncle's eyes. He sees the puzzlement about why his nephew behaves this way.

He knows why.

There is badness deep inside. It keeps the volcano going. He waits for his uncle to get rid of him. It's just a matter of time. He waits and the volcano grows bigger.

Sometimes his uncle feels a volcano too. It is fuelled by his worry, his disappointment and his feelings of failing this nephew who he took in as a young child. He works hard to contain it and fears the day it will erupt.

He sees his failure reflected in the eyes of others. The teachers at school who expect him to get the child to behave; the police who come around when his nephew is missing, again; the neighbours who hear the noise and tell him to make it stop.

He feels the responsibility to his brother to keep this child safe. It's a promise he fears he will break. He doesn't know how much longer he can go on.

Fortunately, the uncle has a spiritual community to support him. They don't judge him. They don't look at him as a failure. They don't try to persuade him that he is a good person for making sacrifices to bring up his nephew. Their quiet support helps to keep his volcano subdued.

The spiritual leader offers him time and space. He listens without blame, without offering solutions, without promises of false hope. He finds he can talk with this man who is so kind and caring.

He tells him of his worry about what the future holds for his nephew who might follow the way of his brother.

He talks of his disappointment that his nephew, like his father, has an active volcano inside.

He admits his feelings of failure, his fear that it's his fault. If he had raised his nephew differently…if he had kept his own volcano in check those times he shouted back, maybe things would be different.

The leader listens. He accepts without judgement all that the uncle tells him. He doesn't reassure or give wise advice. He recognizes how hard the task is for the uncle and how understandable his fears are.

The uncle finds himself telling the leader things he has never told anyone before.

He talks of the upbringing he and his brother had. The racial abuse they experienced when they left the house because of their African heritage. The protection their mother offered and then the tragedy of their mother's death. How they needed to survive in the world alone when their father retreated into grief.

He talks of the different paths he and his brother took: himself into books and learning, his brother into alcohol and criminality.

He talks about the day his brother died and the grief he couldn't show, because his young nephew needed him.

The leader listens. He sits with the feelings. He comforts with few words and much empathy.

And the volcano sighs deeply and rests.

Finally, when grief is spent, the leader wonders, 'Have you ever sat with your nephew like this. Have you ever talked with him about his parents?' He leaves the question with the uncle, no expectation of an answer.

And then the uncle knows what he must do.

He sits with his nephew a few days later. He invites him to talk. His nephew is suspicious, of course. The uncle can feel his nephew's volcano starting to rumble. So, he tells him of his own volcano. His nephew looks surprised. 'You have a volcano too?' and then with passion, 'But yours never erupts. You must hate me, for letting mine out.' His uncle matches the passion as he expresses his sorrow that he hasn't done a better job of helping his nephew to look after his volcano.

An emotional connection grows between them with this shared understanding.

This is the start of many conversations.

At first, they talk about volcanos, and then gradually they start to talk about the nephew's parents.

The uncle talks about his brother growing up. How they had supported each other in a world where they often didn't feel accepted. He also describes the fun they had together and his brother's talent for football, which at last helped him feel he belonged somewhere. With sadness, he tells his nephew how the fun stopped when their mother died, the different paths he and his brother took, and the distance of their father.

The nephew grows courageous enough to talk about his fears that he is like his father. He will also go down the wrong path.

His uncle remembers how the spiritual leader had responded to him. He doesn't reassure or give wise advice. He accepts and has empathy for his nephew's fears. He lets his nephew know he understands. After all, they are not too far from his own.

The volcano inside the nephew quietens, although remains alert.

There is one big fear that has not been expressed. It broods within. This is the most terrifying fear of all. There is a part of the nephew that wants to share this fear with his uncle, while another part shouts 'No! If I tell this fear, all could be lost.' Surely his uncle cannot love a child who carries such evil inside.

The parts argue and the volcano wakes up.

This eruption is big. It wrecks the home with its fury. The uncle almost despairs. His own volcano almost wakes up at another sign of his failure. And then he looks at his nephew, collapsed in exhaustion, the rage spent. He sees a nine-year-old child, alone, desperate and in need of love and care.

The uncle goes to his nephew and takes him in his arms. They sit among the wreckage holding tightly to each other. Finally, they talk about the one thing that they have not been able to speak about. The night of the accident.

The nephew talks about his fear as the car drove faster. He remembers the argument between his parents. And then the car was rolling, and he knew no more.

His uncle continues to hold him tight. He feels his nephew's fear and loss. They sit there absorbing these feelings. He tells him he understands how scary this was. He understands how much he misses his parents, both lost that night.

And finally, his nephew risks all.

Finally, he can hold it in no longer.

Finally, he confesses.

It was his fault. He was to blame for his parents' death. He'd been crying. He couldn't remember what it was about. His parents had been angry with him. His father shouted at him, and then his parents were arguing. That was when the accident happened. It was all his fault.

The nephew cries.

The uncle cries.

The uncle continues to hold his nephew until their crying is done. He understands. A small, confused child who can only make sense of things in one way. He's carried so much blame and shame for all these years.

He holds his nephew.

He holds the blame.

He holds the shame.

And then, the uncle tells the nephew about the night of the accident. His parents had been drinking. For some reason they decided to go out. They took their son from his bed. He imagines how scary and confusing this would be for a three-year-old boy. No wonder he was crying.

The uncle tells his nephew about sitting with his brother as he died. His thoughts were for his tiny son who he'd put in such danger. He tells his nephew that he'd promised his brother he would take care of his son. His father's final words were to ask him to give his son a better life than he'd managed to do.

'I fear I've let you and my brother down,' says the uncle.

'I fear that my badness will drive you away,' says the nephew.

'We will be enough for each other,' they both say.

17

Now You Can ACE It!

Now we have explored the elements of PACE, let's bring it all together again.

First, a reminder.

Playfulness, acceptance, curiosity and empathy provide us with a way of being that creates and strengthens emotional connections. The ACE of PACE work together, allowing us to let others know that we see them, understand them and hold them in our hearts and minds. The playfulness adds an extra element to express our joy in the relationship.

Whether adult to child or adult to adult, PACE creates a pattern to our relationships that is intersubjective, reciprocal, safe and supportive.

REFLECTION MOMENT

★ Is there anything that you would like to add to this summary of PACE?

Take a moment to jot down any thoughts that come to you as you step back and think about PACE as a whole way of being.

This chapter explores the ways the elements of PACE combine to make this whole.

REFLECTION MOMENT

Before you read each section, take a moment to think how you combine the elements when you are being PACEful.

★ Do you have things to add to my reflections?

EXPRESSING EMPATHY AND CURIOSITY

These cousins of curiosity and empathy help us to discover the stories that arise from our experiences. The backdrop of acceptance allows this discovery to feel safe.

If we only stay with empathy, we run out of things to say and are uncertain where to go.

If we offer curiosity without empathy, it can sound as if we are interrogating the other person. We come to a halt again.

> 'The gentle to and fro of curiosity and empathy keeps us moving forward.'

Moving between empathy and curiosity helps us to keep moving forward.

- 'I'm with you. I'll hold you in your struggle when... I wonder what that's like for you?'
- 'I feel how hard it is when... I wonder what is the hardest part for you?'
- 'I feel so sad that this gives you such big feelings. I wonder why you get these big feelings when...'

EXPRESSING ACCEPTANCE FOLLOWED BY CURIOSITY

Acceptance conveys that you get it; you understand the other's experience.

Following acceptance with curiosity helps you to deepen this understanding. This helps you to develop the story that you are co-creating together, the story of the other person's experience.

- 'Yes, it makes sense that it's hard when... I wonder what is hardest about it.'

- 'Of course you would feel confused when... What was most confusing?'
- 'No wonder you got angry when... What do you think made you most angry?'

EXPRESSING ACCEPTANCE WITH EMPATHY

Acceptance is always present. It conveys that we understand the experience of the other. Empathy helps us to show the other that their experience has touched us. We understand and we feel with them.

- 'I understand that this is hurting you when... It is so hard for you.'
- 'I really get that this makes you feel mad. It's so difficult to see...'
- 'I get that you want to do...by yourself. You've been managing these big feelings all alone for such a long time. You're so brave and it's so hard.'

Adding these together we express ACE.

We are hearing and understanding the story of the other person's experience. Telling this story, which has been co-created between us, is a powerful way of witnessing the other. This is what happens when we weave acceptance, curiosity and empathy together:

- 'So, when she...you feel... That makes sense and it sounds tricky. I'm feeling how hard that is for you. I wonder what the hardest thing about it is.'
- 'These are such big feelings, and you're managing them all on your own. For so long you had to manage feelings all by yourself. I'm wondering what is hardest about letting me help you with these feelings.'
- 'I see how thinking that would make you feel sad. That is such a lot of sadness you are holding inside. Any ideas how I can help when you're sad?'

And the story emerges:

- 'I see that this is scary for you. It feels as if it really might happen. You've lived with Mum and Dad for five years now, and each day of those five years you've worried that this is the day when it ends. These parents might find a way to get rid of you, just like your birth parents seemed to do. I wonder why they might want to get rid of you. I wonder what your big fear is. You were telling me that you get very angry sometimes. You know what I'm thinking? I'm thinking that maybe your big anger frightens you. Maybe you fear that if you're so angry then Mum and Dad won't cope. Then you'll have to leave. It's so hard to trust that these parents will stick around. You try so hard to be good and to push down the hard feelings. And those feelings just build and build until they go bang, and then you're scared all over again.'

> 'When we put the elements of PACE together, we truly become storytellers.'

AND ALWAYS ROOM FOR SOME PLAYFULNESS

ACE holds you steady as you build your emotional connection with the other person. Playfulness comes in and out. Finding moments of playfulness helps to build the relationship, lighten the mood and create some joy and togetherness. This is easier for the other to tolerate, when in the past comfort and nurture has been mixed with pain.

> 'Playful moments create space for comfort and nurture to grow.'

- 'Oh, those sneaky feelings, popping up when you don't want them.'
- 'Tell me how that feels?' (*rolls eyes*) 'You know what I'm like.' (*laughing*)
- 'So how big are those feelings right now? Only this big. And here was I thinking they were this big.'
- 'Look in your mum's eyes. See if you can catch her blinking. There she goes, did you see it?'

A PARENT'S MESSAGE TO THEIR CHILD

I hold you in my arms, so tiny, so full of hope. This is my promise to you.

- I will play with you as we find joy in each other.
- I will accept your fears, worries, anger and heartbreaks.
- I will wonder with you, and I will wonder for you when you are not able to.
- I will feel with you, so you know I am with you in all your moods.
- In this way I will find the story that you hold and tell it back to you.
- This is how you will know you are loved.

PACE: THE THERAPEUTIC ATTITUDE

PACE: THE THERAPEUTIC ATTITUDE

Part 3

DDP-INFORMED PARENTING

You will have noticed that in DDP there is a larger focus on the parents than there is in traditional child therapy. Many child therapy models involve the therapist and child while the parents wait outside. Separate time is set aside to talk with the parent, to describe the progress the child is making and to listen to the worries the parents want to share. With DDP, the child work and the parent work are more integrated.

REFLECTION MOMENT

★ What difference does an integrated model of parent support and child therapy make?
★ Can you think of advantages and disadvantages of such integration?

The additional involvement of parents provides the child with a larger environment which is healing for them than the therapy room can provide. On the flip side, it does make approaches more complex and longer than a time-limited therapy.

In Part 3, we explore the home environment provided by DDP-informed parenting. You won't be surprised to see me write that DDP-informed parenting is a slowing down in parenting. Let's think what this slowing down means.

The parent is encouraged to pay more attention to emotional connection and regulation for the child than is usual in traditional parenting. While supporting children with their behaviour is important, it is the emotional connection that helps children to experience safety and trust in parents. This strengthens the connection between parent and child, while providing needed regulatory support. Children are then more able to benefit from behavioural support.

DDP-informed parenting is based on a foundation of PACE, regulation and reflection.

PACE is the attitude that is needed for emotional connection. The parent stays with the child's experience for longer. There is less rush to discipline. Discipline built on understanding, acceptance and empathy will be more effective because the child is helped into a regulated state.

PACEful parenting therefore relies on *regulation*. This is a calming of the internal world of emotions necessary for both parents and child if support and discipline are to be effective. Parents need to be sufficiently regulated to emotionally connect with their child. Children need this regulation when their emotional experience is threatening to overwhelm them.

This approach to supporting children is regulatory based rather than behaviour based. Behaviour is still supported, but this behaviour support is successful because it is based on the child being helped to regulate.

Regulation is successful because it is based on an understanding of the child's experience. This requires the capacity for *reflection*. Reflection is an act of discovery. It is a gentle approach to making sense of what is happening or has happened, and is more effective than a lecture. It helps the child to gain an understanding of their experience with less shame and defensiveness.

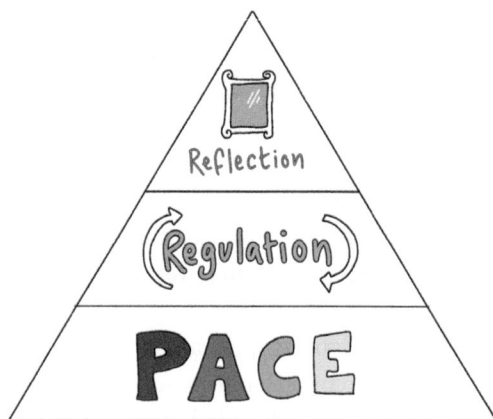

Notice the difference between:

> 'You must not be rude to Mr Scott next door. It's disrespectful and you're old enough to know better.'

And

> 'I understand that Mr Scott unfairly blamed you for throwing stones. I see that would make you feel angry. I feel angry when I get blamed for something I haven't done. I wonder if there's a better way to look after your angry feelings than calling Mr Scott names. Did you notice how that made Mr Scott angry, and then you got even angrier? Let's have a think about different ways you could have managed this.'

PACEful parenting is calmer, gentler and slower.

Traditional parenting has a primary focus on behaviour. PACEful parenting adds a focus on regulation and understanding through reflection. This creates greater safety and security and increases the trust the child experiences with their parent.

18

I Will Be PACEful in My Parenting, Moving Back to This When I Drift

I expect you won't be surprised to know that we're going to start with PACE again. Let's explore how PACE is present when embedding DDP-informed parenting.

> ## REFLECTION MOMENT
>
> ★ What are the benefits when PACE is brought into parenting?

Was your list similar to mine? The PACEful attitude:

- helps the child to become comfortable with emotional connection
- provides co-regulation for the child, so that they can develop self-regulation
- supports the child to manage chores and to cope with discipline.

In the experience of PACE, children know that they are loved unconditionally. And in this knowing, they learn to love themselves.

And yet, PACE is hard.

To be PACEful, we need to be regulated ourselves, managing any trigger points that are challenging us while remaining focused on regulating and understanding the child. We need a good understanding of ourselves and good support.

Even with this in place we will stray. Speaking from experience, I know how the best of intentions quickly get derailed in the face of challenges that a dysregulated child can present. We feel blamed. We feel inadequate. We feel defensive. Our responses to these are often not helpful to the child.

What do you most commonly see, or experience yourself, when parents are struggling with their children?

I think it is blame. I have known parents blame themselves or blame the child. I notice that when blame enters, other things are forgotten.

The parent forgets or dismisses the trauma the child has experienced. They forget that parenting this child is hard because of this trauma. Instead, they protest that they must be doing something wrong, that the child doesn't like them or that the child has some deficiency that hasn't yet been understood.

These are the times when parents need to hold PACE for themselves and to experience it from others. With this support, they find their way back to PACE for the child again.

> 'Like an anchor holding a boat steady during a storm, PACE is there to come back to.'

Let's move a little deeper into parenting. Consider all the tasks that parents do to help their children develop successfully.

Here are three I have thought of:

- *Parents as guides:* Guiding our children to develop as responsible citizens means helping them to take responsibility for age-appropriate chores, cooperating with siblings or participating in family activities.
- *Parents as playmates:* Playfulness is a natural part of family interactions. Parents help their children to engage and have fun.
- *Parents as disciplinarians:* Helping children to manage their feelings and how these are communicated through their behaviours is a parental responsibility throughout their childhood and adolescence.

These are all more difficult for a child who has experienced relational traumas. They spend so much time defensively anticipating danger, that normal family life seems inaccessible.

The offers of emotional connection the parents provide help the child to manage the expectations on them as part of the family.

> 'PACE is my constant, providing emotional connection at play, during chores and when discipline is needed.'

I wonder if you agree that, of these three tasks, discipline is the hardest for parents to manage successfully with their children impacted by relational traumas. The application of boundaries, the need for more supervision than same-aged peers, and disciplining a child who finds emotional connection difficult all pose their own challenges.

Never was PACE more needed. Never was PACE harder to find. Parents deserve support if they are to hold on to PACEfulness around providing discipline.

REFLECTION MOMENT

★ Think of ways that PACE helps a child to manage discipline, boundaries and supervision.

Emotional connection helps discipline feel more manageable for the child.

PACEful parenting regulates feelings of shame, fear and anger in the child so that the child can reflect, experience remorse and want to make amends. The emotional connection also means that the child has the confidence to turn to their parents to support them with this.

- *PACE before discipline* helps children to feel emotionally connected.
- *PACE with discipline* helps to maintain this connection when the children are at their most vulnerable, experiencing shame, fear and anger.
- *PACE following discipline* provides the children with a continuing sense of being unconditionally loved, repairing any ruptures in the relationship.

- *Connection before, during and after discipline* teaches socially appropriate behaviour while maintaining safety and trust.

Discipline provided from within a connected relationship teaches the child to behave in socially responsible ways. It helps the child to know that mistakes and poor choices are recoverable, and relationships can be repaired. Connection helps parent and child to collaboratively discover logical consequences that help this repair.

As you have noticed, I like the anchor analogy for parenting. An anchor represents strength and steadiness, and these are very much things we need in parenting. PACE and emotional connection are an anchor for parents to hold on to as they guide, support, play and discipline their children impacted by relational traumas.

SO YOU KNOW THAT YOU ARE LOVED

I will be PACEful with you. And when I stray, as I will because this is hard for both of us, I'll find my way back to you.

In this way, you will know that you are loved.

I will stay PACEFul with you when family life is too hard, when expectations just feel mean. I'll be there to support you.

In this way, you will know that you are loved.

I will offer PACE so that we can learn to be playful together. In fun we will discover the joy in our relationship.

In this way, you will know that you are loved.

My PACE will be the cushion that softens discipline. This will be hard for you. Our emotional connection will make it easier.

In this way, you will know that you are loved.

And when your emotions get too strong, when you're excited, or frustrated or angry, my PACE will calm your emotional storms.

In this way, you will know that you are loved.

This will take time. It will be hard to believe in the love that I offer. I'll be patient.

PACE will be our anchor, and we will weather the storms together.

In this way, you will believe that you are loveable.

19

I Will Hold Our Relationship Close and Cherish It

I'm sure that you appreciate how important a child's relationships are. This is especially true of those relationships which provide the nurture, love and care that children need to thrive. Parents, grandparents, close members of the community all hold a special role in the child's life.

It is the responsibility of these caregivers to help a child to feel loved, valued and special.

We describe this as unconditional love. For healthy development, there are no conditions which dictate whether a child will be loved or not.

REFLECTION MOMENT

★ Think about the challenge of combining love with other parenting tasks, including teaching, guiding and disciplining.

It is important that children don't experience a withdrawal of love as part of teaching, guidance or discipline. There will be restrictions on the child's behaviours; there will be rules the child is expected to follow, and the child needs discipline and boundaries. Love, however, does not disappear from healthy relationships when these conditions are applied.

The adult also takes responsibility for relationship repair. Difficult times are inevitable. The child might be extra challenging, the parent might have external challenges making them less available or there are simply ruptures in the relationship because the parent cannot be available at a time of need.

Whatever the circumstances, the nurturing parent will notice that a rupture has occurred and will actively repair this rupture with their warmth, kindness and concern for the child.

Boundaries still apply; discipline is followed through; apologies are made when a parent has not been available. All of this is needed within a warm, loving relationship.

You might, like me, be thinking about times when you have felt especially challenged by your child or a child you are supporting. At these times, it can be hard to like the child. However, deep down our love for them continues, and we find ways back to it. This is what a child needs from us. This is the unconditionality of the relationship.

- 'I will love you no matter what.'
- 'I will protect this love even when I'm struggling to be with you.'
- 'I will find a way to help us back to this loving relationship when times are hard.'

> 'It's always my responsibility to nurture my relationship with you.'

With developmental trauma come additional challenges. We are parenting a child who does not trust relationships and who does not believe they can ever be unconditionally loved. Imagining themselves as a monster, they find it hard to trust what the parent is offering.

This often leads to more challenging behaviours as children protest, reject, cling to or test the relationships they are being offered.

Those parenting the child can find it hard to find and hold on to their unconditional love in the face of these challenges. However, this is what the child needs most.

REFLECTION MOMENT
Reflect on what parents need to get through difficult times.

★ What are your top two?

Were yours the same as mine?

For me, the first is support. However, it can be hard to seek support when we feel as if we are failing, struggling or not wanting to continue.

Are you someone who tends to turn away from support when it is most needed?

This is when non-judgemental support is most necessary. It is important to ensure that parents of children impacted by relational traumas come into parenting knowing that they will need and deserve support. If not, they may not pick up the phone when most in need.

Second on my list is taking breaks. This is easier to say than to put into place, especially when a child is challenging and offers of help are few and far between. Parenting is an ongoing task. If a parent is to stay in it for the long haul, they also need times to rest and recuperate. Breaks are a way of protecting the relationship. Opportunities for breaks is a must for those parenting children impacted by relational traumas.

Never have children needed relationships more than when they have experienced hurt and loss of relationships. My hope is that we live in societies that make this possible.

'It is at the hardest times that the child needs parental love most.'

THE THREADS THAT CONNECT

Mishal had always been aware of the thread that connected her to her daughter, Dania. Even while the umbilical cord was being cut she knew that this thread continued. It was a thread that was nourished by the deep love she felt for Dania. It was a thread that she could hold on to at times of challenge or worry. It was a thread that thickened when they shared closeness together in their relationship. It was a thread that vibrated with colours when they found moments of joy together.

As Dania grew, there were the usual trials of parenthood, moments when the thread thinned and frayed a little. The thread also needed to stretch as Dania found her feet and went out into the world. The thread, however, was strong and it sustained through all the ups and downs of childhood. Mishal and Dania had a deep connection expressed within an environment of unconditional love.

When Ameera came to live with them, Mishal immediately knew it was different. Ameera was the child of a distant relative whose circumstances meant they could not care for their daughter. Mishal, supported by the whole family, willingly took Ameera in. She dearly wanted to love Ameera as her own, recognizing how much she needed this. The thread was not there though. This felt different.

Ameera could be challenging, and Mishal understood the fear and grief she was carrying at the loss of her parents. It was, however, hard to soothe and nurture a child who expressed this fear and grief in anger and rejection. Mishal, having no thread to hold on to, found herself becoming angry and rejecting in turn. Mishal needed to find a way to create a thread that could hold them together – a thread that would provide the connection that she experienced with Dania.

Mishal remembered the solidity of the thread in her parenting of Dania. She discovered it in the gaze she focused on her small infant, in the delight she experienced with each developmental achievement, in the reconnection when they had tough moments together, and in the connection that did not break when Dania was away from her. How could she create this with Ameera?

Mishal realized that she needed to find new ways to create a thread to connect her to Ameera.

Mishal gazed at Ameera when she slept, noticing the beauty in her face when it relaxed and feeling the responsibility to keep this child who had suffered so much safe and protected.

Mishal paid attention to Ameera's achievements, finding ways to notice and celebrate these even while Ameera dismissed their signficance.

Mishal paid special attention to small moments of joy that she and Ameera experienced together. These might come and go quickly but she savoured each one as the precious moment it was.

When Ameera needed discipline, Mishal remembered to provide this with warmth and understanding. She ensured that some connection was maintained even while she needed to enforce a boundary.

When Ameera was angry and rejecting, Mishal steadied herself in remembering that she was a good parent, doing the best she could. In this way she met anger with understanding and rejection with warmth.

When there was disconnection between them, Mishal ensured that she reconnected with Ameera as soon as she was able. She let Ameera know that the relationship was strong and would continue to be there for her.

And when Ameera did not believe in the connection between them, Ameera let her know that she would believe for both of them, protecting it for the day when Ameera would believe in it too.

And when Mishal could not do any of these things because her emotional reserves were depleted by the sheer unrelenting nature of Ameera's needs, she gratefully accepted her sister's support. This nourished her so that she could in turn nourish and strengthen the fledgling thread that was forming between herself and Ameera.

Day after day, year after year, Mishal attended to this thread so that Ameera would get the connection she needed. What had been easy with Dania was more challenging with Ameera, but Mishal knew that this made finding ways to connect even more important.

Many years later, Mishal sits with Dania and Ameera, now grown and parents themselves. The grandchildren play nearby. And as she sits there, Mishal is surrounded by threads. She watches these threads glow with many colours. She marvels at their thickness and sturdiness. She smiles at the knowledge that these threads connect them all, and will endure through generations to come.

20

Curiosity Opens Our Eyes to Your Experience

I want to return to curiosity again.

We all come to PACE in different ways. Some find strength in empathy and that in turn opens up their curiosity and acceptance. Others find different beginnings.

I wonder what your beginning is.

Curiosity is often my way in, especially when empathy and acceptance feel a bit depleted. If I can hold on to my curiosity, I find increased understanding, which then opens the door to the rest of PACE.

> 'In curiosity I see the world differently.'

I remember the time I first noticed the power of curiosity. It was such a simple moment, listening to someone on the radio talking about the beauty of a tree in winter when all the leaves had dropped. Suddenly I looked at the winter trees in a totally different way. Whereas they had previously left me with a touch of regret that summer was past, and winter was on the way, I now noticed the beauty in their shape and the majesty in their structure. The simplicity of the radio programme had awakened a curiosity in me that made me look at the world in a different way.

REFLECTION MOMENT

★ Can you think of a moment of recognizing the power of curiosity?

So, what happens when we are not awake to our curiosity?

I notice how my actions are dictated by my assumptions, whether right or wrong. I move quickly to action or reaction. I jump into finding a solution before I have truly understood the problem.

Does this sound familiar?

Here is an example my son experienced when a teacher failed to be curious. He was around seven years old and was generally enjoying school. He had a lively intelligence and was keen to learn about the world. However, the teacher was frustrated with his writing. He felt that my son was not trying hard enough. He needed to put more effort into the writing activities. My son tried to please the teacher, but his writing did not improve. One day, perhaps in frustration that the writing was not improving or perhaps the teacher was having a particularly difficult day, he took my son's attempts and threw them in the bin, telling him to try again. My son put down his pencil and refused. It was a long time before he tried writing again.

While I have been curious about the teacher's motives when retelling this story, I was not very curious at the time!

Can you see the failure in curiosity of this teacher?

REFLECTION MOMENT
Think about what stops you being curious.

★ How do you find your way back to curiosity again?

We talk a lot about slowing down within the DDP model. When we act fast, we don't leave space for curiosity. We jump into action. Ironically, this speed can slow us down in finding a helpful way forward. Or perhaps we move into despair and come to a standstill. Either way, slowing down and making room to be curious will help us gain a new perspective and hopefully help us to find a way forward.

> 'When I delay action and stay with curiosity, we both understand what has happened.'

Let's think about the example above and see how slowing down might have changed the outcome.

I'm sure you've noticed that there was no curiosity about why a seven-year-old boy might struggle to write. In my son's case, he was severely dyspraxic, which made fine motor movements very tricky. He had years of teachers complaining about his writing until we found a wonderful therapist who designed a writing approach for him based on the movements he could do. A little curiosity and understanding of the difficulties that he struggled with led to a helpful solution in the end.

Curiosity opens a window to the world of experience. And to stretch the analogy a bit, the window can then help us to find a path forward.

THE DOG WHO REFUSES A WALK

Most dogs love walks, and this is true of Bramble. She is a beautiful five-year-old retriever who anticipates her daily walk with excitement bordering on the hysterical! If you've ever known a retriever, you will get the idea. Each day she and her owner walk down the lane to the local park. Here she enjoys a run around and the opportunity to exercise her nose. She discovers exciting smells everywhere.

It is a surprise therefore the day that Bramble refuses to walk down the lane. They get halfway and she simply stops and whines. The owner can see no reason for this. There are no changes in the lane, and there are no other people around. He tries to encourage her on, but to no avail. He tries to walk back the way they came but Bramble just sits and whines. In the end a very frustrated owner half carries, half drags Bramble home – not easy with a 30kg dog who does not want to move!

The next day the same thing happens.

The dog trainer suggests some tasty treats to encourage Bramble. Nothing changes.

The vet checks Bramble to see if there are any physical problems that are making her uncomfortable. She has a clean bill of health.

The owner is at a loss. He could try a different route, but this lane is very convenient for the park. Bramble just won't move past this same spot.

At last, with nothing working the owner goes to the lane and stands where Bramble stopped. He looks around but can see nothing unusual. He looks at the fence on the right, but Bramble has never been worried by a fence before. He looks at the hedge on the left. It is an ordinary hedge. He then notices a shed on the other side of the hedge. Curious, as this is the exact spot where Bramble stops. The shed is on an allotment which runs down the side of the lane.

The owner fetches Bramble and takes her to the allotment. Eagerly, Bramble pulls him over to the shed. It is an ordinary garden shed, but not to Bramble. She sniffs and paws at the door, looking at her owner repeatedly. She fusses and whines, clearly wanting to get into the shed. A gardener working on the adjacent allotment comes over to see what the fuss is about. She tells them that the shed belongs to a man who has been confined to bed for the last few days. She offers to go and talk to him, to see if he is willing to let them open the shed so that they can discover the source of Bramble's anxiety.

Can you guess what they find when she returns with the key and opens the shed?

It's a cat, hungry but otherwise no worse for her confinement!

The owner wonders how Bramble knew the cat was there. Had she smelt something or heard something? He would never know, but he remained curious.

21

Understanding Is Always Kinder Than Judgement

In the last chapter, we explored curiosity and how it leads to deeper understanding. We are now going to build on this to think about how understanding is more helpful than judgement.

> **REFLECTION MOMENT**
> Think about a recent difficult relationship.
>
> ★ What made it hard for you to be non-judgemental? What helped you?

Meeting someone with non-judgement can be very difficult when we are challenged by their behaviour or despairing of their mistrust.

I wonder how many times you have judged someone today. The driver who cuts you up on the road; the neighbour who fails to smile as they pass by; the child who refuses the dinner you have lovingly cooked.

> 'I strive to make sense of your experience so that I don't react with judgement.'

Judgement is an inevitable part of living alongside people, and of course judgement is involved in raising children.

- We need them to understand right from wrong and so we judge their behaviours.
- We want them to have success in life and so we judge their school achievements.
- We want them to enjoy healthy relationships and so we judge their friendships.

When we make such 'judgements' with an attitude of PACE these will be delivered in a context of warm acceptance. We strive to understand and accept the experience that underlies the behaviours. We hold a non-judgemental attitude towards the wishes, beliefs, thoughts and feelings the child holds. Our judgements now feel like guidance.

REFLECTION MOMENT
Reflect on a time with a child.

★ Note all the things that you do or say that show judgement.
★ Note all the things that you do or say that show guidance.

And of course, this brings us back to slowing down.

In slowing down, we move away from lecturing the child. Instead, we take the time to show we understand through the discovery of the stories of their experience.

Notice the difference between:
- *Telling a child that they must not run into the road (lecture).*

and

- *Taking the time to notice with them their excitement at seeing the neighbour's dog being taken for a walk; how much they want to pet it and how in their desire they forget the rule that we mustn't run into a road (story).*

Can you see how in the second one the adult is staying with the child's experience so that the child feels understood? The child is then more open to listening to the adult's worries about running into the road.

> 'When a child experiences our understanding, our judgements become guidance.'

Judgement is a complicated experience. It can reduce the other's feelings of security and safety with us. It always needs the context of understanding, acceptance and empathy if we wish to guide someone successfully.

TWO BROTHERS

Clyde and Sammy shared some difficult experiences together. Born into neglect and violence, they had huddled together for comfort. Clyde, the older by two years, did his best to look after Sammy but he was only little himself. Hunger and cold were the backdrop to their first few years. Sadly, their parents, victims of their own early life experience, could not make the changes needed. It was a courageous decision to agree to the boys moving to adoption, made in the hope that they would have a better life.

It was a difficult transition. Just four and two years of age, Clyde and Sammy were too young to really understand what was happening. They did know that everything had changed. It was nice to be warm but the sounds, smells and space were all different. The boys continued to huddle together for comfort. Clyde continued to try to look after Sammy. He watched these new parents, strangers still, carefully, making sure that they were not harming him, and although he ate voraciously, he always made sure he put some of his food on Sammy's plate.

Gradually, the strangeness became familiar, and the boys settled in. Trust developed more slowly, especially for Clyde. He became quite bossy, insisting that he oversee Sammy's bathtime and bedtime; he still made sure Sammy had enough to eat, and he fussed when they went out, worried about all the dangers that could befall his younger brother.

When Sammy started school, Clyde had more worries. Would the teachers be kind to Sammy? Were the other children letting him play?

Gradually, Clyde relaxed, supported by the teachers' understanding and his parents' patience. Clyde developed strong friendships, a passion for drama and he took pride in caring for the rescue dog who had joined their family. The two shared a difficult start in life and it created a strong bond between them. The adults relaxed as they experienced Clyde's increased trust in them.

It was a surprise therefore, when, aged eight, Clyde began picking fights with the other children. The teachers called the parents in for a meeting. They considered how to provide increased supervision. The teachers outlined the consequences they were putting in place. They discussed introducing Clyde to a nurture group which would emphasize kindness to each other. The parents expressed their anxiety that Clyde might be 'going the way of his birth family'. Could his early experience of violence be impacting him? It was a worrying time. They sat Clyde down and made it very clear that violence was not acceptable in their family. They told him that if it continued, they would not be able to trust him to take care of the dog. Clyde protested that he would never hurt the dog. He appeared contrite and promised not to fight any more, but three days later it happened again.

The teacher running the nurture group had a chat with Clyde's parents. She observed what a kind and caring boy Clyde was. The fighting seemed very out of character. He was still doing well in school, enjoying his friends and his drama. Was anything going on at home that could be unsettling him? They couldn't think of anything. Driving home, his parents started to wonder. Why had this fighting begun? There seemed no obvious triggers. The fights were with two boys, both younger than him. Why these boys?

When they sat down to talk with Clyde, they approached it differently. They noticed all the ways that Clyde was kind and caring. They commented on how good he was with the dog. They observed how protective he was with his brother. They wondered why he needed to fight with the two boys.

Clyde's head went down, and he remained quiet. The parents wondered with each other. They wondered why a boy who was kind and caring would start fighting younger children. They noticed how much Clyde cared for his younger brother, and how good he was with the younger children at the drama group. Still Clyde was quiet.

They suggested they make cups of drinking chocolate and fetch some biscuits to keep them all going while they figured this out. Clyde cuddled into them, drinking his chocolate and eating his biscuits. They let him know that it was all right. Whatever it was they were there for him. They wondered if the boys had been mean to him. Clyde shook his head and started to cry. He tearfully told them that the boys were not mean to him, but they were mean to Sammy. They teased him for being adopted and they told him he was a baby because he sucked his thumb. He hated those boys for being unkind. He didn't want to hurt them, but he wanted to make sure they stopped.

Now it made sense, Clyde was protecting Sammy, as he had always done. They let him know that they understood. Of course, he would be cross with the other children if they were being mean to his brother. They were sad that it was hard for him to let the adults help. They then gently told him that the fighting had to stop. This wasn't the way to sort out a problem. They would help him; together they would figure this out. They would talk to the teacher, and they would all find another way to protect Sammy.

Clyde felt his trust growing as he experienced the warm support of his parents and teachers. He didn't fight the children again.

22

I Nurture Your Dependence So That You Can Grow to Be Healthily Independent

Infants are born fully dependent on caregivers.

As I write this sentence I am reminded of the popular saying: 'It takes a village to raise a child.' This has become a common observation which originated in Africa. It is an Igbo and Yoruba proverb, existing in many different African languages, and reflects the importance of a wide range of people in a child's life. It rests on the belief that a child is best raised with the collective involvement of a community.

I wonder what community you were brought up in.

Sadly, in Western society it is not uncommon for a family to be quite isolated from their community. Increased social mobility, the importance of career, achievement and independence and the loss of extended family can all contribute to this isolation.

I am starting with these reflections as I feel they provide an important context when thinking about dependence and independence.

It seems self-evident that we want children to move from total dependence to some form of independence. What may be less obvious is what we mean by independence.

REFLECTION MOMENT

★ What does independence mean to you?

Socialized in a Western society, I value the importance of career and achievement, alongside healthy relationships and family. Perhaps with this emphasis I have lost something in the raising of my children which African and other indigenous cultures remind me of. This is the value of being part of a social group, of collective responsibility. I imagine in societies that stress the importance of the group, independence holds a different meaning. Children are raised to be responsible for giving back to the social group. This seems less important than achievement in Western society.

As we think about helping children move along a path from dependence to independence, we can keep this in mind. Let's stay thoughtful about what independence we want for the children in our communities and let's be mindful of the meaning of independence to ourselves and respectful of the meaning of independence for families we are supporting and interacting with.

In whatever way we think about independence, what is universal is that the growth away from total dependence is partnered by emotional maturity.

Think about your own emotional maturity. Is it something static that you fully attained as an adult or is it moveable, weaving between more and less maturity, dependent on what is happening in your life, your health and current stresses?

Do you notice that we can be more or less emotionally mature from day to day?

Emotional growth is not a straight path. It weaves and meanders as we grow from dependence to independence. Our children can appear all grown up on one day and then in need of more support the next. We adjust the support we give to accommodate these varying needs.

If you are caring for or supporting a child impacted by relational traumas, you have likely noticed that this variance is more obvious and dramatic. Emotional growth is not a smooth path for these children.

> 'I remember that while your chronological age advances with time, your emotional age is constantly in motion.'

The work of Stephen Porges[1] highlights how emotional growth is dependent on the amount of rest, relaxation and restoration we get.

Think of the traumatized child and notice their hypervigilance, their poor sleep patterns, their struggles to calm and regulate. They are not getting the rest, relaxation and restoration that they need. Their emotional growth suffers. It is no wonder that they are emotionally younger than their same-aged peers, and that their level of emotional maturity fluctuates within and between days.

This can create problems for the child, especially if we have age-related expectations of what they should be able to do.

Additionally, if we are working or living within a culture that expects children to grow into independence quickly, the child will be under pressure to meet expectations that are unrealistic for them.

These expectations are further increased when the child is mixing and going to school with same-age peers. The pressure to be like and keep up with these peers can be strong, especially as the child is moving towards adolescence. The need to 'grow up fast' is challenging for both child and parent.

Have you heard someone worrying about allowing a child to be dependent on their parent?

Certainly, in the UK where I live this is a common concern. There can be fears of 'babying' a child and that by meeting their dependency needs we are somehow slowing down their ability to be independent. In my experience, children are more likely to make developmental progress when their dependency needs are met.

I once met a group of adoptive parents who were all sharing anecdotes about their children's desire to be a baby. Some pretended to be baby animals, others wanted to be given a baby's bottle to drink from. All but one of these parents had resisted these behaviours out of a desire to help them 'be their age' and fit in with their peers. They were frustrated at the persistence the children showed in 'playing babies'. One of the parents had allowed the child to explore their needs to be younger.

Guess which child grew out of these needs fastest?

You won't be surprised to know that it was the one who had been allowed to explore their infantile needs.

1   Porges, S.W. & Porges, S. (2023) *Our Polyvagal World*. New York: W.W. Norton & Co.

> 'Independence develops when dependency needs are met.'

It is therefore important to be aware of the child's level of emotional maturity and to adjust expectations in line with this. This is important both at home and school. This can be challenging with the day-to-day demands that are made on parents and teachers, but if this isn't done the child experiences increased stress. We can all testify that when stress goes up our level of maturity goes down! By expecting too much we can increase the challenge for both child and adult.

Have you noticed how supervision and discipline also need to change with fluctuating levels of maturity?

Children need increased structure and supervision when emotional immaturity is high, and can cope with more freedom when maturity increases. The adult therefore needs to provide the structure and supervision needed based on emotional needs in the moment.

Getting this right can reduce the need for discipline. When consequences are piling up it is a sure sign that the child is struggling emotionally.

Empathy and acceptance alongside structure and supervision can help the child find some emotional balance again.

REFLECTION MOMENT
Imagine an old-fashioned set of scales.

★ What would you put in the left-hand pan to help you know that a child needs more nurture and closeness?
★ What would you put in the right-hand pan to help you know that a child can manage more freedom and responsibility?

The word balance sums it up.

If we find the correct balance between need for dependence and independence the child will make faster developmental progress towards emotional maturity.

It is a balancing act as needs fluctuate throughout the day.

THE BALANCING ACT

The elder was a great age and had been providing this service for a long time. In the community, they were respected for their wisdom. The elder's job had been their parents before them and their parents before that. It was now time to pass this on to their own younger kin. They were one of the Scales in the community, helping others to find the right balance in the bringing up of their young.

The Droo lived in a land far away from here. They were human-like and yet not human. Most of them had large hands and feet and round bodies. The Scales, in contrast, were tall and thin, with two arms ending in hands in the form of pans.

Independence   Dependence

The Droo lived in social groups, each having a specific role in the community. Bringing up the young was an especially respected role. Much like human children, the children of the Droo grew up at different rates and had variable need of their caregivers.

The caregivers valued their ability to know each child and to recognize what they needed. The Scales were an important part of this knowledge. Each youngster was brought to a Scale each morning. The Scale would talk to them, observe them and then their arms would find the balancing point between the two pans to indicate what the child needed for that day. If the balance shifted to the left, it let the caregivers know that the child needed to be kept close, their dependency needs catered for. If the Scales shifted to the right, then the child was able to manage more freedom and responsibility within the community.

One of the young, named Mood, was the special responsibility of a new Scale, Ode. Mood was a delightful Droo, full of fun and mischief. However, they did have some struggles. Born early, Mood had been kept alive by the skill of the Birther. Mood was left with some struggles, including the challenge of managing their emotions. Some days, Mood needed a lot of help, whereas on other days they seemed to manage better.

Ode was struggling. They used all their skills of observation taught to them by the elder. They asked all the right questions and yet their Scales could not find the right balance point.

The caregivers were getting frustrated. They cared about Mood and wanted to get things right for them. Yet some days Mood raged at the restrictions on them. They didn't want to stay close to the caregivers. On other days, Mood was expected to play with the other young and to carry out simple chores, but they squabbled with their peers and forgot to do the tasks given to them.

Ode noticed Mood getting more and more dispirited. Mood became convinced that they were the naughtiest Droo of all, and their emotion was more up and down than ever.

Ode sought the elder for advice. What could they do to help Mood so that they could be the fun Droo they were born to be, able to be mischievous and responsible, finding their place in the community?

The elder asked Ode to take Mood to them. The elder spent time with Mood, observing them and asking many questions. Finally, they felt they knew enough. The scales were balanced heavily to the left. They brought Mood close to them and helped them to know that they were special in the community. They had a special part to play in bringing fun and laughter to the Droo. However, they also needed some special help. Mood needed to be patient while the caregivers took care of them. Mood might not be able to do everything the young ones were allowed to do as they needed more time being taken care of. Mood needed the care missed out on when they were newly born and very poorly. 'Be patient, Mood,' they said. 'You'll have freedom, and you'll take on responsibilities, but we need to take care of you first.'

The elder instructed Ode in the careful observations they needed to make. They cautioned Ode to go slowly and allow the pans to move to the right in their own time. Mood would get there if they were given the support they needed. And when Mood felt frustrated at not making the progress of the other young, Ode should be extra caring. Ode should let Mood know that they understood how hard this was, and take them to the elder if they needed some time away from the community.

Ode took special care with their observations. They supported Mood to manage when the restrictions felt too hard, and they took it slowly so that Mood was successful in the steps they were taking.

The elder looked on with pride, knowing the community was in safe hands. Ode became the most skilled Scale of all, and Mood fulfilled his role to bring fun and laughter to the community.

23

My Authority, While Kindly Meant, Is Hard for You

Parenting has many aspects to it. Just pause for a moment and consider all the things that parents do for their children.

Do you agree that the parents' primary responsibility is to keep the child alive?

The infant is born immature and completely dependent on the care they are offered. Providing a safe, healthy home is a priority.

Beyond this the parent is a developmental guide, providing the child with the stimulation and experience needed to help them develop successfully. The world they provide starts small and then widens out in line with the child's developing maturity.

Of course there are many responsibilities within these two areas. I want to focus on two aspects of parenting and explore how the child manages these.

Broadly, parenting can be seen as falling into two roles.

The first involves authority. Parents need to be in charge, deciding on the structure and boundaries to the child's day. The parent says when it is time to get up, time to eat, time to go to school, time for leisure (including how much screen time to allow!) and time to go to bed. And of course, parents manage the fallout when the child disagrees! While the growing adolescent might get some say in these things, parents are in charge until their young people become adults ready to leave home.

The second surrounds the stimulation that parents provide. Essentially, they are playmates, engaging the child in experiences and activities that they enjoy. This is good for their development as well as providing emotionally connected experiences.

'I will be playmate and authority figure and transition between these carefully.'

Do you notice the difference between these two roles? Think about who is in charge.

In authority, the parent is taking control. They decide on the rules and boundaries. The trusting child might protest but they believe in the parents' good intentions.

As playmate, there is a more reciprocal relationship. The child has more control over the play. At times, the parent follows the child's lead. In fun, the child is also happy to follow the parent's lead. This is a 'to and fro' experience.

REFLECTION MOMENT
Reflect on a typical day for a young child.

★ How much time is spent with the adult in charge?
★ How can the adult make this easier for the child?
★ How much time is devoted to reciprocal play?
★ How can the adult help the child manage the transition from play to authority?

The trusting child will move easily between the parent in play and in authority. With a gentle reminder that the transition is approaching, they cope with ending a game.

REFLECTION MOMENT

How do children impacted by relational traumas respond to parents in authority and in play?

When we bring mistrust into the scene we see a very different picture. Children manage states of mistrust by taking charge. Feeling in control feels safer than waiting for whatever they imagine the parent is going to inflict on them. Mistrusting children struggle with authority as it means relinquishing control.

When a parent uses their authority to keep the child safe, these children often revert to controlling behaviours.

Harder still is ending play. In play, the child can happily boss the parent around and choose whether they want to follow the parent's ideas or not. So, what happens when the game ends and the parent uses their authority again?

I expect you can imagine the scene. This is not in the child's game plan. They do not want to give back control and they push back hard against the instructions for what is happening next. For these children, the transition from the parent as playmate to the parents as authority figure feels unbearable. These relational transitions can lead to very rapid shifts towards anger and meltdown.

The parent needs to find a way to stay open and empathic to the children's struggles in letting them have a benevolent authority over them.

'I remember that my parental authority feels unsafe for you. I can help you to manage the transition between our playfulness and my structure and boundaries.'

CHANGING TRACKS

Boiler loves his job. He likes nothing more than taking the children on rides along the track. As a steam train, he enjoys working with Driver. Driver gets him ready for the day. Cleaned and polished, he waits eagerly for the first children to arrive. Driver jokes with him as they fill the firebox with coal. The children climb on board and Boiler glows with pleasure at the excitement they are bringing.

At Boiler's signal, Driver sounds the horn and they are off. Boiler knows the way and needs very little help. He lets Driver know when he needs more coal. They are a good team, Boiler and Driver. The day ends with a final wipe down and Boiler settles down in his shed.

Then one day, it all changes. Driver arrives as normal, but she is not her cheery self.

'We have different work to do today,' she tells Boiler. 'We have to take some goods to the next town.'

Boiler is dismayed. Why is today different? He misses the sounds of the children arriving for their ride. And then Driver tells him they don't need to do the usual polishing.

'But I like being polished,' Boiler protests.

'No time,' says Driver. 'We've lots to do today. We need to get these goods on board and move onto the other track. Those points are always sticky – let's get a move on.'

Boiler's firebox is filled with coal in record time and reluctantly he starts up. He doesn't even get to signal Driver to sound the horn. They go a short way down the track and then Boiler is brought to a stop. This is where they change tracks and it all feels very confusing. There are no excited children. There is no fun with Driver. Boiler is not happy at all.

Boiler goes more and more slowly. Without fun with Driver and the excitement of the children, Boiler can't find the energy. Driver feels frustrated. She puts in more coal, but it's no good; Boiler is not making the effort needed.

Driver brings Boiler to a halt and checks him over. Everything seems in good order. There is no reason to account for the lack of speed. Driver decides to eat her sandwiches while Boiler has a rest. As she eats, she wonders what the problem is.

Boiler is sorry. He wants to help Driver. He understands that it is important to get the goods to the next town. It's just so unexpected, and he feels out of control. They don't feel like a team any more.

Driver has an idea.

'I'm sorry this was sprung on you,' she says. 'Of course, it's unsettling when everything changes without warning. I need to make sure we do this delivery, but I need your help. Tell you what, you tell me when to sound the horn and when you need more coal, just as you usually do. I need to show us the way, but we're still a team. Tomorrow we'll be back with the children again.'

Boiler feels better. Driver understands why this is hard for him.

'Let's go,' he says. 'Sound the horn!'

Boiler and Driver get the goods to town and Boiler even enjoys the return trip. Driver makes sure he is clean and tidy when they get back. She tells Boiler that there will be other times when they must make deliveries because one of the other trains is out of action. She promises Boiler that she will warn him next time.

Boiler feels happier as he settles into his shed. They've done a good job today and tomorrow the children will be back. He and Driver are a team, but he understands now that sometimes Driver needs to take charge.

24

Parenting Combines Discipline With Warmth and Nurture

We have been exploring how the DDP model can inform the parenting of the child impacted by relational traumas. Much of this rests on the attitude of PACE. This way of being creates safety and security, helping the child to trust in emotional connection.

Do you remember when you first encountered the idea of PACE as an attitude?

It sounds very appealing and deceptively simple. Putting it into practice is a different matter. We want to connect with the children but there are roadblocks in the way.

The children may resist this connection, pushing back as they try to stay in control.

The children may cling to the connection but are never soothed by it.

And of course, children need guidance and discipline, which can disrupt connection.

REFLECTION MOMENT

What do you think is most challenging when parenting children who struggle to connect?

When I consider this question, I return to the feelings around failing – that sense of not being good enough or not being the right parent for the child. These feelings get easily evoked when a child resists the emotional connections we offer. They become angry and challenging when we provide reasonable consequences and boundaries.

Parents need two hands for parenting, providing both connection and behavioural support.

- *Hand one* holds the warmth, nurture, fun and curiosity, while the attitude of PACE helps the child to feel safe and secure.
- *Hand two* provides structure with appropriate boundaries, supervision and discipline. When this is done with an attitude of PACE the child can experience continuing emotional connection.

> 'A lack of emotional connection as an infant makes it difficult to connect when older.'

Building an initial connection with a child beyond infancy when they also need structure, supervision and discipline is challenging. It can leave child and parent feeling not good enough. As Jon Baylin and Dan Hughes[1] have described, the child becomes blocked in their ability to trust, and the parent blocked in their capacity to care.

Parents also need two hands holding them so that they can keep offering their two hands of parenting despite the challenges being presented. The emotionally resilient parent with loving support surrounding them is more able to attend to their two hands of parenting.

REFLECTION MOMENT
Reflect on your two hands.

- ★ What do you have in each?
- ★ What do you need in other people's hands to support you?

The two hands work together so that the child can get the parenting they need in an atmosphere of security, warmth and nurture.

---

1   Baylin, J. & Hughes, D.A. (2016) *The Neurobiology of Attachment-Focused Therapy.* New York: W.W. Norton & Co.

And in case this sounds impossible, remember it is all right for parents to get things wrong, to have bad days or to run out of emotional capacity when the child has been particularly demanding. Parenting is never perfect and relational repair, led by the parent, can help parent and child get back on track.

I remember spending a day with a group of foster carers describing to them DDP-informed parenting. One of the carers became very dispirited. 'I'm doing it all wrong,' she told us. 'I'm not sure I'll ever get this.' I paused to think how I could respond helpfully when a foster carer nearby turned and said to her, 'It's okay, love, you've always got relationship repair.' The foster carer beamed. 'Yes,' she said, 'I think I can do that.'

There is a popular game where the players can get sent to jail. Sometimes they are holding a 'get out of jail free card' which they can use to get back into play. I think of relationship repair as a 'get out of jail free card'. I know I have used plenty of them while parenting my two children! With a stack of these cards ready, I can offer two hands of parenting, knowing I can use them on those occasions when I drop a hand, or two!

> 'My two hands hold you safe, my two arms embrace you. In this way you experience discipline with warmth and nurture.'

TWO HANDS FOR PLANTING

The orchard is not thriving. The saplings were planted at the right time, and the weather has been favourable, but the trees are not growing tall and strong as they should. Fruit is in scarce supply, and this does not bode well for the Guild of Food Providers.

The orchard is the responsibility of Idrina, the youngest acolyte in the Guild. Idrina is a complex individual, born at a time of much stress for the Guild. Times are better now but Idrina still carries the burden of those difficult times. There are days when she is loving and giving, with a lightness to her step and a song in her heart. On other days, it's as if a dark cloud has descended. She is quick and methodical, but there is a hardness to her; something unyielding in her way of being.

The others have learned Idrina's moods. They have learned to leave her alone when the clouds are down and, in this way, they get on well with her. Alissa, the chief Provider, is concerned though. She likes Idrina, even has a soft spot for her. She cared for her when times were at their darkest, but if Idrina cannot help the orchard to thrive then she will not be able to stay as part of the Guild.

Alissa decides to spend time with Idrina. She wants to observe her at work. Maybe she will see what the problem is. Idrina is happy to have her company and is cheerful in her work. For a few days Alissa watches Idrina tenderly planting the saplings. She moves quickly from one to the next, offering kind words and a gentle touch as she puts the sapling into the ground. In no time, she has two rows of saplings planted. All seems well.

The next couple of days see a change in Idrina. The dark cloud is on her. She continues to plant the saplings, but her touch is brisk and there is no song. She pauses at each one, pushing a stick into the ground and roughly attaching the sapling to it. This is a slower process and only one row is planted.

Alissa thinks hard about what she has observed. She knows the moods of Idrina and can see that they affect the way she works. She wonders if this is the reason for the orchard not thriving. Alissa goes to look at the saplings planted during the previous season. She can see the neat rows, carefully planted by Idrina. In the first two rows the trees have grown but they do not look healthy. They are not tall and strong but bent and withered. The next row is different. These trees have grown taller, but they still don't look healthy, tethered tightly to the sticks beside them.

Alissa realizes what the problem is, and she has an idea to fix it. She calls Idrina to her and gently holds her hands.

'You have two strong plant-growing hands here,' she tells Idrina. 'I can see how you use them as you plant the saplings.'

Idrina is intrigued. 'What do you see?' she asks.

Alissa holds Idrina's right hand. 'I see this hand so tender and loving. With this hand you give the saplings the warmth they need. However, this hand is quick. It doesn't take the time to provide a stick for support or water for growth.'

Alissa then takes Idrina's left hand. 'This hand is different. It provides the saplings with what they need but is less caring. This hand provides a stick for support and water for growth, but the warmth is missing. These saplings are not getting the tender loving care of your right hand.'

They walk the orchard together and Alissa points out the difference in the rows of trees.

'I see now,' says Idrina. 'I'm using one hand, when the saplings need two. The saplings planted by my right hand are not getting the support they need while the saplings of the left hand are not getting enough care. I need to use both my hands together.'

Alissa claps her own hands with pleasure. Idrina is perceptive and she's right.

'I think,' said Alissa, 'I've not been paying enough attention to my hands. You have days which are harder, when the cloud surrounds you. On other days you're lighter, and the sun warms you. You need my hands to hold you steady through these changes. Then I think your two hands will work together and the saplings will get everything that they need.'

And indeed, this is what happens. Idrina learns to know her own moods and to ensure she gets the support she needs. Her two hands become as one, working together to create the best orchards in the land, producing healthy, strong trees yielding the sweetest of fruits.

DDP-INFORMED PARENTING

DDP-INFORMED PARENTING

Part 4

DDP-INFORMED PARENTING SUPPORT

Part 4 is a bridge between Part 3, which focuses on DDP-informed parenting, and Part 5 on DDP as therapy. We explore the support parents need to help them with parenting and to prepare them to be involved in their child's therapy.

When you reflect on the DDP model, I wonder what you see as its unique features.

For me, it is that DDP is so much more than a therapy approach for children.

As I see it, all the adults in the children's lives are an integral part of helping a child to recover from trauma. If adults are essential for recovery, then they will also need to be included within DDP approaches.

REFLECTION MOMENT

★ Who do you think are the important people to involve in DDP approaches?

My list includes:

- Education staff involved in the child's schooling.
- Social workers supporting the child and parents.
- Community leaders offering much-needed support.
- Health practitioners who look after the child's physical and emotional health.

Above all, is the central role that parents play in the lives of the child. All parents – birth, foster, adoptive, kinship, residential, respite – will be part of the equation that makes a safe and healing environment for the child to grow up in.

Here we focus on supporting parents. Parents need help to understand the DDP model and the therapy that will be offered to the child, with their support.

Whether or not the child engages in DDP therapy, the parents are offered:

- an opportunity to reflect on themselves, their past relationship experiences, and how these impact on their parenting of the child

- an understanding of DDP-informed parenting and support, so that they can adapt their own parenting styles to incorporate the DDP principles

- an opportunity to explore their own parenting values, their heritage and any past intergenerational trauma that might impact their parenting. They will discover with the DDP practitioner how to adjust their parenting within the context of this experience

- an opportunity to explore their child's current and past experience, including any trauma and current experiences related to their heritage, culture, sexuality, gender, class, health, neurodiversity and religion that might intersect with their past

- ongoing support to continue these reflections, to manage times of crisis or difficulty, to help them when they move into blocked care (a biological consequence of parenting children who struggle to be parented, which impacts on their capacity for caregiving), and to be part of the community of support all parents need and deserve.

As you will see from this list, DDP cannot be described as a short-term approach!

While episodes of therapy for the children may be time limited, support for the parents is not. DDP is like the elephant in the image, supporting the weight of what the parent is doing for the child.

I believe that parents who undertake the task of parenting children impacted by trauma deserve ongoing support. No one should be alone in parenting. We all need supportive communities around us. For parents of traumatized children, this support can drift away in the face of what can be overwhelming needs and challenges presented by the children.

DDP practitioners are part of these communities and need to be in it for the long haul.

You may have experienced people who worry that we are making parents dependent on us when we offer long-term support. This is not a concern that I share. I see support as helping the parents to be autonomous, healthy and resilient, enabling their children to move happily into adulthood and beyond.

25

A Child's Fear Can Lead You to Doubt Yourself

In this chapter, we think about parenting challenges.

First, take a step back with me to consider relationships and how they work. Even as we take this step back, there is another step we have missed. Why do we need relationships?

Think about our development as social creatures. This development served many purposes. It helped us to cooperate, to work together, to take care of our immature young.

Can you see how all this requires relationship?

> 'Relationships are the heart of what it means to be human.'

Are you a social person, thriving on company, or do you enjoy solitude? I lean towards the latter. But wherever we fit on this continuum, we all need others.

I remember a child I was working with who always tried to persuade me that she didn't need relationships. She would make it on her own. And yet, when I wondered with her how she would enjoy being stranded alone on an island she was horrified at the idea. This horror was not about surviving, finding shelter, searching for food to eat, avoiding being eaten. It was about being alone.

We all need relationships. This doesn't mean that relationships are easy. We work hard to gain and to sustain our relationships.

Think about the relationships that you enjoy most.

My guess is that these are the relationships where you gain most and can give back. The reciprocity of relationships is what nurtures us. The relationships we find most difficult are those where it is hard to give, and you get very little back.

So, back to parenting challenges.

REFLECTION MOMENT

★ What are the hardest parts of parenting?

There are many things we can struggle with. I expect we all have our own list.

Keeping our children safe; helping them to be healthy; supporting them to grow, develop and be educated. All these things can be stressful. We keep on doing it for the love of our children.

These are hard, but are they the hardest aspects? Again, it comes down to reciprocity. As with all relationships, the hardest part of parenting is with a child who takes little from you and gives little back.

Children may find reciprocity hard for many reasons.

For example, disabilities can impact on how well children can give and receive. This can be challenging for parents. Understanding the struggles the children have can help parents maintain empathy for them or find their way back to empathy when it is lost. These parents can find a way to have a rewarding relationship with their children, and to relish the moments of triumph as the child takes another step forward.

Developmental trauma brings another twist to this tale of parental challenge.

'You didn't cause your child's hurt, but parenting reminds them that they were hurt.'

When children have experienced fear, terror and/or loss of parents they are impacted in several ways:

- They miss opportunities to learn how to be part of reciprocal relationships.

165

- They learn not to trust in their parents.
- They learn to defend against anticipated danger and abandonment.

These hard-won lessons are with them as they move into new homes. A child, frozen in time, rests within them. This inner child watches out for the next danger but cannot distinguish the present from the past.

Being parented presents the biggest fear of all.

REFLECTION MOMENT

Reflect on the ways a child shows fear of being parented.

★ What is it like when a child fears you because you are the parent?

My list includes:

- Resisting reciprocal relationships.
- Needing to stay in control.
- Rejecting the parents, as they pull them in and push them away.

The child feels safer, while the parent is left wondering what they are doing wrong and why they cannot reach this child.

I have often experienced how parents of children impacted by relational traumas enter a world of failure and self-doubt. It is hard to keep offering what the child needs when this is met with fear, silence and pain, and yet without this the child cannot learn to leave their past behind and to trust in the present.

It is a long road, and these families deserve support to find the resilience they need. DDP approaches are part of the package of support offered to the family.

THE DAY THAT LIFE CHANGED

The dog could have been attractive. He is of medium build, nicely balanced and with a heritage that offers the best from a mixture of breeds. Time has taken its toll, however. His coat is dull, his eyes too alert and he bears the wounds of many fights.

He has no memory of his beginnings, one of a litter removed from the mother too early, handled roughly and with little care. He left as soon as he was strong enough. He has learned to live on the streets. He roams with the packs of street dogs. He has learned which dogs to stay close to and which to avoid, but this knowledge has not been acquired without the fights that left him bruised and scarred outside and in.

He has no memory of his beginnings, but the past lingers anyway. It shows itself in the caution he shows as he scavenges for food. It shows itself in his vigilance, ever ready to fight or flee. It shows itself in the way he keeps his distance from the humans he shares the space with.

And then his life changes forever.

It begins as any other day. He leaves the comfort and protection of the dogs he's spent the night with, the freezing temperatures having overcome their caution as they curled together for warmth. He needs food and so he circles his usual haunts. The back of the bakers where stale bread is often discarded. The dustbins that overflow, making easy pickings, even the river bank can sometimes give up a stranded fish. Today is not his day. The baker's yard has been tidied, the bins have been emptied and the river bank is frozen.

The dog roams further, wary of strange dogs that he has not encountered before. Without knowing it, he strays into an area where patrols are circuiting; they are part of a charity, rounding up the street dogs and finding homes for them.

This is how his life changes.

Hunger overcoming caution, he finds himself caught and caged. Fear overwhelms him as he snaps and bites any human that comes near.

Days, months, years follow. He is moved from one kennel to another, never trusting the humans that try to take care of him. He is shipped abroad where the sights, sounds and smells overwhelm him with their strangeness. He is homed, rehomed and rehomed again. He can't trust in each new caregiver, and in despair they hand him back.

Options are running out at the final kennel he is taken to. There is, however, something behind his fear and hostility. Something that attracts the attention of one of the kennel staff. His coat is shiny from the improved care. The wounds are healing and the scars are hidden beneath his thick coat. He has become a handsome dog.

And on the inside?

His eyes remain alert and wary, but behind the aggression and the aloofness there is something else. A fragment of the dog he was meant to be: a gentle soul ready to be a loyal companion.

And so his life changes one last time.

He has found someone with the patience, skill and perseverance to keep on trying.

He has found someone with enough support to keep going, even when it feels as if their efforts are failing.

He has found someone whose unconditional love wakes up the unconditional love that he has to offer.

He will never be the dog he could have been. He will always need careful handling. The desire to fight or flee is never far away. However, happiness is his. He brings joy to his new owner, and is able to receive moments of joy in return.

26

It's Hard to Trust in Your Goodness When Your Child Tells You Otherwise

As we explore many times in this book, it's hard to be a parent of a child who does not want to be or does not trust in being parented. The need of the child to defend themselves can emerge in rejecting or clinging behaviours.

These can lead the parents to doubt themselves. Carrying a sense of failure, they develop their own defences.

> 'When I feel a failure, all I can do is defend myself.'

I wonder whether as a parent or in other ways have you ever doubted yourself? I guess most of us have at some point in our lives.

> **REFLECTION MOMENT**
>
> ★ What do you do when you experience periods of doubt?

Here are some possibilities:

- Blame others to avoid blaming yourself.
- Demand actions from others as you experience the fear of not having actions to take yourself.

- Go round and round in circles, looking for a fix to the problem.
- Be angry with others as you try to suppress the anger you feel for yourself.

You might also have tried to support someone who is demonstrating these defences, often bringing a sense of discomfort.

REFLECTION MOMENT

★ When supporting someone who is defensive do you notice any similarities in how you respond to them?

The responses can be very similar:

- Blaming and avoiding them.
- Providing lots of guidance, which never seems to be followed.
- Joining them in a futile search for answers that don't exist.
- Feeling angry with them for making your life difficult.

Dan Hughes struggled with these same things when he was developing DDP. He understood the importance of support and noticed how hard this could be with some parents. He persevered, recognizing the importance of holding empathy for the parents at these times.

When we move away from blaming, judging and offering futile guidance, we start listening to the struggles the parents are having. As we listen with acceptance and empathy, the parents relax their defences. They allow us to see their vulnerability and our empathy increases. Then we can work together to find ways to support them and their child.

But how do those of us who are practitioners move away from damaging judgements so that we can find this empathy?

Dan discovered an answer for this as well. As practitioners, we go into our relationship with the parents holding three assumptions.

1. These are good people.
2. They are doing the best they can.
3. They love their child or really want to love their child.

> **REFLECTION MOMENT**
> Think about the three assumptions.
>
> ★ What makes it hard to hold the assumption and what helps you?
> ★ What differences do you notice when you hold these assumptions?

In holding these assumptions, we explore the stories the parents relate to us differently. We lose our judgements and join them in their struggles. We are a shoulder to cry on, a port in the storm, a place where they find the calm needed to reflect and discover.

> 'Support helps you discover who you are and the person you want to be.'

These reflections are not just about the child. The parent also learns about themselves, their strengths, their resilience, their wisdom. And the most important discovery of all: 'I am a good person. I am doing the best I can. And I love this child.'

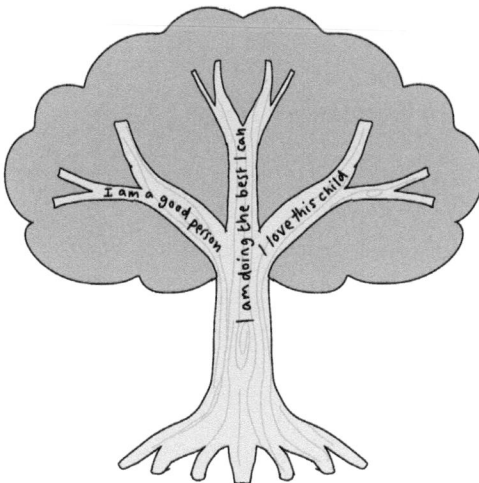

And if you are a parent, maybe it will help to hold these same assumptions about those you are interacting with. Challenging as this is, especially if you are feeling judged and blamed, these assumptions help to build a relationship on mutual trust rather than distrust.

WHO AM I?

'Who am I?' I ask.
'I don't know,' you say. 'Let's discover together.'
'I'm a failure,' I say. 'Not the parent I hoped to be.'
'I understand. Let's discover this parent you imagined.'

And you take me by the hand and lead me on a voyage of discovery.
We board a ship and travel to worlds I was afraid to visit.
You are always at my side, holding me when I falter.
I see the parent I want to be and grieve that my child rejects this.
I see the parent I have become and am bathed in your lack of judgement.
I confront the parts of me that lost hope. You hope for me.
I see the child my child could have been and grieve the loss of this child.
I see the child my child has become and finally understand why.
I see the parent and child that we could be together, and you rejoice with me.

'Who are you?' you ask
'I'm a good person,' I say.
'I'm doing the best I can.'
And 'I do love my child.
Help me to remember this when I forget.'

27

It Is a Challenge to Be Needed When You Need Distance

You know those parenting times which feel extra challenging? Maybe the child is being more oppositional than usual. You are juggling several things at once and perhaps not giving as much attention as needed. Stress builds up for both of you.

These are the times when an explosion becomes more likely and harder to prevent. At these moments it feels as if you are the worst parent in the world, and your child is the most difficult.

For those of you who are parents, does this sound familiar?

At that moment, what you need most is to move away. You need some distance from the child who, like the cactus, has spines that threaten to hurt you. You need time to calm and regulate. The irony is that these are the precise times when children need closeness.

The reconnection after a rupture lets the child know that they are loved no matter what. Without this repair the child becomes more anxious. They experience themselves as bad, and their parents as not loving them. The ultimate fear is that they will be abandoned, and this fear of abandonment is terrifying.

> 'It is at challenging times that children need connection most.'

In good enough parenting, the child is soothed, a reconnection is made, and these instinctive fears subside. All is well again.

Consider this for the children who have experienced relational traumas.

There are additional layers of complexity that stem from the children's experiences of abuse, neglect and loss. These children are experiencing the rupture in the present while also being impacted by unresolved ruptures of the past.

This presents additional challenges:

- The child's meltdowns can be longer, louder and more extreme.
- The child may need to reconnect but will also experience high anxiety about reconnection linked to feelings of not being good enough.
- The child displays this as ambivalence or rejection: 'I want you but I'm not sure how it will go. I'm not sure that I want to find out.'
- The child's fears of abandonment are rooted in their previous experiences of being abandoned.
- The child needs and fears connection. They demonstrate this in increasingly challenging behaviours.
- The parents need distance to restore their own equilibrium. This increases the fears of the child.

And round and round it goes.

REFLECTION MOMENT

Reflect on a time when someone needed you but showed this in ways that were challenging.

★ Notice how your body responded and the thoughts that came up.
★ Notice how you felt towards the other and how you felt towards yourself.

When feeling threatened by their child's behaviours, parents may become angry, rejecting, punishing – a range of behaviours to protect themselves. Notice that this is a biological response directed by part of the brain known as the amygdala that is responding to the perception of threat.

Defensiveness breeds defensiveness and both parent and child, although needing connection, move more deeply into disconnection from each other.

> 'Defensiveness is an appropriate response to threat; it helps us to survive.'

Within DDP approaches, we recognize the importance of helping the parent to move out of their defensive responding to reduce the escalating arousal that is occurring. We know that if the parent remains open and engaged, the child calms more quickly. This in turn helps the child to develop trust in the parent, 'You will be there when I need you most.' They will also experience increased trust in themselves. 'Maybe I'm good enough and you won't abandon me.'

We know the problem. We know what is helpful. How can we help the parents to stay open and engaged at times when their biology is crying out for defence?

REFLECTION MOMENT

Consider who you want support from when you are feeling defensive.

★ How do you want to experience their bodily state and how does your body respond to this?
★ What thoughts do you want them to hold and how does this impact on your thoughts?
★ What do you want the other to feel towards you and how does this impact on how you feel towards yourself?

Support from others has the potential to help parents move out of survival mode.

When the child is threatening the parent with hurt and rejection, the parent needs to be kind to themselves and let others help. This can be a challenge. Feelings of failure can lead the parent to withdraw from support.

It is also difficult when others do not understand the challenges the child is presenting. Parents can find that their normal support drifts away at these times.

Support from a DDP practitioner who understands the difficulties can increase the resilience of parents. Parents then remain open to connecting with their children, even at the hardest times.

> 'Support can move us from surviving to thriving.'

THE PARENT'S TALE

I love you with all my heart, and yet it is not enough. I see your stress building and I notice my stress responding. I am powerless to prevent the meltdown that I know is coming. It seemed so trivial to me, and yet for you it is so much bigger. I know I'm not responding well. Your stress feels like anger, and I'm the target. It's not personal, I do know that, and yet my body responds to defend against an attack. My anger feeds your anger. We're going nowhere fast.

I need to move away. I need time to calm myself and then I can support you. You do not allow this. You follow me around. It feels provocative and despite myself I respond. If only you would give me space I could help you, but space feels threatening to you right now. You need me and yet you're pushing me away.

I focus on my breathing as I try to control the emotion that is threatening to overwhelm both of us.

I remember my supporter, who understands without judging. I picture their kind face and gentle voice, and I feel myself calming.

It is enough.

I now focus on my voice. I try to match your intensity. I remember acceptance and empathy. I put my reasoning voice away and you start to calm. Finally, I'm hearing you and I see you relax. 'Now you're getting it,' you seem to say. Am I, I wonder? I feel drained, emotionally spent.

I stay with you though.

We reconnect because I love you no matter what.

28

Parenting Traumatized Children Can Trigger Our Own Past Hurts

We live in the present while planning for and worrying about the future. Our past sits behind this, there to reminisce about, but rarely do we notice its subtle presence on our everyday existence. It's strange to think about how much our past can influence the present.

How we were raised, the relationships we have had, the experiences we encounter. This all sits within us. We move forward in the present, but we do not leave our past behind.

Our past can give us resilience. We learn, we adapt and we move forward taking these lessons with us.

This experience can also lead to vulnerability, pressure points that are ready to be prodded. We react, often without awareness of the influence of the past.

We think we are dealing with something that is current and live, and yet part of our reaction is because of something past and long gone. If we stop to consider this, we notice that our reactions are irrational or extreme. It takes a little bit more thought to work out why this is so.

Does this sound familiar?

I noticed how much I reacted to my teenage daughter at certain times. She would say or do something, and I would respond like a bottle of pop. You know, the kind that explodes if shaken too much. This was not good for our relationship, but I couldn't make sense of my strong reactions. It was only after considerable thought that I realized that my daughter was unwittingly talking to me in a way that resembled my sister. The more difficult part of my relationship with my sister was being triggered. My reactions, evident in my response to my daughter, were in a strange way also a response to my sister. My angry feelings from the past towards my sister were being played out with my daughter. Unfortunately, a consequence of this was that I was not able to notice what my daughter needed. I was not available to her, and you can imagine the difficulty this created.

It's complicated, isn't it?

REFLECTION MOMENT
Think about moments when you suspect past and present collided.

★ Notice what belongs in the present and what to the past.
★ As you separate these, notice how this feels different.

It gets more complicated still when we bring a child's trauma into the mix. A child arrives with their own past in place ready to be triggered. They view their current relationships through the lens of their past.

- A parent says no to them, and they view the parent as mean and scary.
- A parent asks them to do something, and they perceive a threat.
- A parent leaves them with a babysitter, and they imagine they will never see them again.

So, consider the toxic mix when both child and parent are being triggered at the same time.

A child is having a tantrum over some slight event, maybe not being allowed to have something they want. The child is responding to the disappointment in the present. 'I want it and am frustrated that I can't have it.' The child is also responding to fears of the past. 'When I feel frustrated, I get beaten.'

The parent in turn is experiencing the tantrum as a child's frustration in the present while also having a huge sense that they are failing as a parent, stemming from childhood messages that they will never be successful.

The child needs support to regulate the extreme emotions they are feeling.

The parent is dysregulated by the invasion of the past.

They both retreat into defensive responding, and you can imagine the rest.

> 'When past relationships enter, we end up in confusion, managing past and present at the same time.'

I hope from these examples you see the importance of having a good understanding of the impact of past relationships, especially our attachment relationships.

REFLECTION MOMENT

Reflect on exploring your past relationships with someone.

★ What did you find helpful and what was threatening or exposing?
★ Is there anything different you would have liked from the other person?

DDP practitioners spend considerable time with the parents exploring their attachment history and understanding the influence of the past. This can feel exposing, but it is not just idle curiosity or nosiness on the part of the practitioner. The focus is always on current parenting. 'Let's understand how your past impacts on your parenting. Let's especially pay attention to those triggers that are hard to manage.'

As a parent understands their reactions, they find it easier to regulate themselves in the present and thus to be available to their child when most needed.

> 'Exploring attachment history builds resilience to potential triggers. We can remain present to the children when they need us most.'

THE CLASH OF PAST AND PRESENT ON A PARENT-DAUGHTER RELATIONSHIP

Mae's childhood was a mixture of absence and pushiness. Her mother, suffering with depression, loved her children but had little emotional energy for them. Her father wanted his daughter to be the best, the fastest, the brightest. Approval came with achievement. It wasn't an unhappy childhood. However, it was a childhood within which there was a pressure to succeed for her father and a need to be careful around the fragility of her mother.

Kali's early childhood was one of neglect and absence. A single mother preoccupied with the next fix, and moving from one unsatisfactory relationship to another. Kali spent some time in the care of her grandparents, but they were preoccupied with their own problems, not least the inability to reach their daughter who had emotionally departed many years before.

Foster care gave some relief for Kali, who appeared to thrive during the nine months she was there. No one noticed the grief and loss in the child's eyes as she did her best to please these new parents of hers. When she was moved to live with Mae, she was four years old.

Kali did not understand what she had done wrong. She had been abandoned twice in four short years – at least that is how she experienced it. Gone was the compliant child of foster care.

Kali was told that these were her 'forever' parents. She didn't know what forever meant. All she knew was that parents left eventually. She was determined to do things her way. She would not need these parents, and she would not miss them when they left.

It was a hard start. Mae did her best to demonstrate to Kali that she was loved, and she was safe. Kali did not appear to be interested in these messages. She was tense, watchful and demanding. Mae felt on permanent trial, and it was a trial that she was failing. She tried to meet her small child's needs.

- How do you meet the needs of a child who does not signal what they need?
- How do you soothe a child who seems determined to let you know you are not what they want?
- How do you feed a child who does not want to be fed?
- How do you dress a child who throws the clothes down in temper?

Mae was told to give it time. It was early days, she would settle. Days turned into weeks, weeks into months and months into years. Kali's opposition to her mother only grew stronger and more vocal. Nothing her mother did was right. By the time she moved into adolescence they were both at breaking point.

Let's pause in the story and consider what was happening between these two.

Kali was living with the certainty of loss. In all the actions of her mother she saw neglect and indifference. The template from her birth mother overlayed her experience of her adoptive mum. As Mae became increasingly frustrated the certainty became an inevitability. Any day now, it was just a matter of time. Kali redoubled her efforts not to let her mother in. She would not experience emotional connection. She could not bear the loss if once she experienced it.

Mae was living with the certainty of failure. She could not parent this child. Kali would not connect with her because she saw what a hopeless mother she was. When she looked at Kali she saw her father's eyes looking at her. His disapproval and disappointment were evident in every frustrated response from her daughter. His insistence that she do better was in every fresh demand that Kali made.

Can you see that this relationship is not a straightforward one of mother and daughter? It is a relationship which includes a daughter's mother and a mother's father.

And so, let's continue this story of endurance, disappointment and some successes.

Mae had strength. She persevered even while she despaired. Despite the frustration, despite the constant failures, she loved this child with all her heart. She would not abandon her. She held on. Each time her frustration got too strong and impacted on how she responded, she sought to reconnect. She found her way back to empathy for Kali by remembering her sad history and holding on to the knowledge that somewhere inside Kali was a little girl ready to be loved.

And Kali, she was strong too. She knew that she needed her mother but was determined not to show this. She had a longing to belong. She suppressed these longings for fear the disappointment would be too much to bear.

The longings were there, though, deep within, and sometimes despite herself they rose up. She made a gesture towards her mother, a gesture of need, a gesture of love. Then she was frightened all over again and her demands and anger redoubled. Mae doubted that the gestures were ever there at all.

They could not survive this alone. Each of them needed the support of those outside their dyad. Kali had a therapist who worked with her and her mother. Together they found moments of connection and together they helped Kali to understand her early experience and the longing and fear that it had left her with.

And Mae had the support of her husband, Kali's adoptive father. He stood by them both, lending strength where he could. He had his own story with Kali of course, but this is not part of our tale today.

Mae also had the support of the therapist. They understood without judgement, holding on to hope when hope was low. They absorbed disappointment and failure while holding on to the strength and successes that neither Mae nor Kali could hold on to themselves.

This family journey was by no means an easy one, but it was survivable. Kali lived with them until she was old enough to leave. She went out and tested herself in the world while her parents could only hold their breath. It was a rollercoaster journey, but eventually, Kali could appreciate that she had a family for life. She recognized the hard times she had put her parents through and understood why she had to do this.

This was enough. Kali found stability with her parents and stability to live alone. She had a family who supported her, and this gave her the strength to create a new family, where she is now a good partner and mum. I'm not talking about happy endings; this is real life. There are ups and downs, but Kali no longer needs to do it alone.

29

When Parenting Becomes a Job and Closeness Feels Unbearable

As all parents know, there are times when the joy of parenting deserts us and parenting is a very unsatisfying job. Sometimes these slumps in parenting are an outcome of additional stresses in our life. Sometimes our children are being extra oppositional or uncooperative and our resilience is low.

> 'When I feel no joy in parenting, it is hard to be close to you.'

Our commitment to our children keeps us going through these times. We watch them when they sleep and remember how innocent and vulnerable they are. They do something which is kind, and we experience a surge of love for them. Parenting feels joyful again.

Do you recognize this? You might find it helpful to understand the role of biology.

Parenting is closely linked to hormonal changes.

When we are feeling close and loving with our children, we experience oxytocin, the feel-good hormone. As oxytocin increases, we feel closer to the child. We enjoy the interactions we are having, and this triggers another hormone, dopamine. This is the reward hormone.

When oxytocin and dopamine are flowing, we want to be close to our children and parenting feels rewarding.

This also impacts on the way we view our children. We can read our child accurately, and our meaning-making, understanding what is going on for our child, is realistic.

The child is fussing because their sandwiches are cut the wrong way and we have given them the wrong juice. We remind ourselves that the child has had a busy day coping with visitors. They are tired and this is making them extra fussy.

There are days, however, when the relationship with the child just feels off. We are not experiencing the reciprocal loving interactions, and our oxytocin and dopamine become depleted.

Now closeness to our child feels unpleasant. We would like some distance from them. The way we read our child and our meaning-making become distorted, often by the implicit beliefs we hold about ourselves. We forget the busy day and the visitors, and instead we experience the child as out to get us, and ourselves as a failing parent.

In the previous chapter we explored how our past can impact on our present. It is these past relationships that distort the lens we view our child through at these times of extra stress. The off button has been pushed on our caregiving systems and we are viewing ourselves and the child at our most vulnerable.

Let's bring the child's trauma into this picture.

Children who have experienced relational traumas are very wary of entering into reciprocal relationships. If you have parented or supported a child with this experience you will know how controlling they can be within their interactions. Control is a great way of avoiding reciprocity. The child feels very comfortable influencing others but does not trust enough to be open to the influence of another.

> 'Care can become biologically blocked when children hurt and reject us.'

It is the reciprocity between parent and child that provides the emotionally connected moments which support the caregiving systems. Without this, these systems switch off.

Dan Hughes and Jon Baylin[1] describe this as 'blocked care'. The parent is not getting enough back from the child, and this takes its toll.

---

1   Hughes, D. & Baylin, J. (2012) *Brain-Based Parenting: The Neuroscience of Caregiving for Healthy Attachment.* New York: W.W. Norton & Co.

REFLECTION MOMENT

★ Have you experienced blocked care, in parenting, supporting or teaching children, caring for a relative or supporting an aged parent?
★ Reflect on how this felt in your body. Notice the thoughts you had. What feelings arose within you?
★ If you have supported someone in blocked care you might review these reflections as this impacted on them.

DDP practitioners need to recognize these states of blocked care so that their approaches can be adapted to help the parents. The parents are not getting nourished in their interactions with their children. They can be helped if they are nourished by their relationships with others who understand without judgement and offer acceptance and empathy. This helps them find their way to acceptance and empathy for their children again.

When parents move out of blocked care and remain emotionally available to their children, the possibility opens that the child can begin to trust in their parents' care and therefore move into reciprocal relationships with them.

REFLECTION MOMENT

★ What do you think are the qualities needed when supporting someone in blocked care?

> ★ What thoughts, feelings and bodily states are needed to pro-
> vide the support required?

I LOVE YOU, BUT I DON'T WANT TO BE NEAR YOU

Preparing Jani for the school trip is a trial of love. The school is doubtful that she will manage the two days, which include a night away from home. They fear her dysregulated outbursts, which will be harder to manage out of school.

Jani wants to go, and Hart and Nicky, her adoptive dads, really want to make this work. Jani already feels different from her peers on so many levels. She is adopted. She is the only child in her small school with two dads and she is emotionally immature compared to her classmates. School is tough. The emotional outbursts when she gets home after a day of managing the demands and expectations on her testify to how challenging this is.

Jani wants to go on the trip and her parents really want to make this happen.

Hart bears the brunt of this. He is supported by Nicky, but he is the one to do the negotiations with school.

Hart is the one who creates the story about the school trip, in an attempt to help Jani know what to expect during the time away. He hopes reading this story will give Jani enough familiarity to help her feel safer with the many changes she will be managing.

Hart is also the one who takes the brunt of Jani's anxiety as the trip gets closer. Jani always verbally attacks Hart when her stress levels increase. Hart is exhausted by these preparations.

Hart perseveres and Jani does go on the trip. Not only does she go but she manages to cope with everything. Of course, this does take its toll, and Hart and Nicky know that there will be some pay back when she arrives home.

Hart puts down the phone with a sigh. One of the teachers has called to let him know that Jani has done well. They are now on their way back to school and there have been no major problems. Jani has joined in with the activities with the additional support in place and has even cooperated with the other children.

There was one difficult moment when one of the other children teased her for having two fathers. Fortunately, Jani's supportive adult talked with Hart ahead of time about how to manage this, and they navigated this successfully. It even presented an opportunity to talk about all the different family situations children can have and for Jani to notice that all children had their own unique family.

Hart mentally prepares himself for collecting Jani. He thinks about how to greet her, what they should do on their return, how they will navigate bedtime with the level of tiredness Jani will be experiencing. He sighs again.

Nicky notices this and is curious. 'Why the sigh?' he asks. 'It sounds as if it has gone well thanks to all your hard work.' Hart thinks about this. He notices a hollow feeling inside. Where is the pleasure he ought to be feeling at the success of all their preparations? Why isn't he looking forward to having their little girl home? Why can't he muster up the energy to begin preparing Jani's favourite supper?

Hart realizes that he doesn't want Jani to come home. He feels no pleasure in her return, just a sense of dread settling inside him.

'Am I a monster?' he asks. 'I love Jani, but I really don't want to be near her just now.'

Nicky pulls Hart towards him. He doesn't judge. He doesn't reassure. He recognizes these feelings and really feels for Hart. 'I'm with you,' he says. 'We'll get through this together.'

30

Don't Tell Me What to Do. If It Were That Easy, I Would Have Done It

I wonder what you think about when you hear the words 'parent support'.

Parents might be expecting parenting advice, or maybe they fear they will be judged for their parenting.

> 'Parents need support more than they need unhelpful solutions.'

I'm sure you appreciate that DDP parent support does not judge. There will be some parenting advice, based on understanding the experience of the parent and of the child. Beyond this, DDP approaches seek to emotionally connect and support.

This is a collaborative approach to providing parent support. The practitioner and parent work together to figure out what is going on and to find ways to successfully parent the children. This approach to supporting parents requires a lot of slowing down.

REFLECTION MOMENT

Think of the phrase: 'Going slower to get there faster.'

★ What does this mean to you?

Within the DDP model we believe that slowing down gives us time to explore and understand. This helps us to make more progress than a quick search for solutions.

I'm reminded of Aesop's fable of the tortoise and the hare. It may not be the original meaning of this unequal race between animals. However, the tortoise's slow, steady pace wins the race despite the hare's speed. Can you see a parallel here?

As Jon Baylin told us during the DDP conference in Nottingham, UK, in 2024, we need to 'move from fast and furious to slow and curious'. So much of life is fast and furious, this slowing down can feel challenging and uncomfortable. We are not used to moving at a slower pace.

> 'When I'm fast and furious I don't see you. As I slow down to be curious you come into sharper focus.'

When we have time to understand the experience of the parents, it deepens the parents' understanding of themselves. This self-reflection enriches the understanding of the child and from this, solutions, or at least things to try, emerge.

> **REFLECTION MOMENT**
>
> ★ What strengths and what challenges do you experience in going slower?
> ★ How do we go slower while also managing the rush of daily life and the expectations on ourselves?

If the practitioner and parent move too quickly, this may be because they are feeling defensive.

- The parent may be defending against feeling judged and blamed. They conceal their vulnerability to avoid the pain of feeling a failure.
- The practitioner may be defending against feeling they should have all the answers. They rush to reassure, offer solutions without understanding, or focus on the child to avoid a focus on the parents.

Can you see how going slower to move behind these defences allows support for these most hurt parts?

The DDP practitioner needs to:
- have less focus on immediate problem-solving and advice-giving and more focus on curious exploration
- understand the parents' experience of parenting the child
- understand the impact the child has on the parent. It can be helpful to understand this in the context of previous attachment history and relationship experience.

Notice the DDP model in these interactions. The practitioner and parents discover the stories together. These can be stories of successes or failures, of frustrations, doubts and worries. They can be stories of the past as it impacts on the present. They can be stories of hope.

Can you see how this slowing down parallels the work with the child?

The DDP practitioner works with the parents in a similar way to which they work with the children. This is emotionally supportive and helps the parents to get an impression of how they can be with their children.

So much in DDP is about modelling the model.

I wonder what slowing down as a DDP practitioner looks like to you. Here is the process as I understand it:

- Connect PACEfully with the parents and explore how things currently are.
- Help the parents to consider the impact on them of the experience they are having with the child. Explore and co-regulate any experience of shame, anger, fear and despair this brings up.
- Explore the current ways of supporting this child in the context of past relationship experience. Co-create new meanings for the parents about their reactions to the child.
- Use this understanding to inform ways that the parents might try to emotionally connect to and support the child.
- Consider the challenges that the child is presenting. Gain some understanding of these based on the child's current and past experience and explore parenting strategies that might help to reduce these challenges.

As you can see, this is not a quick process. It can be frustrating for parents who are living with day-to-day difficulties and challenges, when they are hoping for quicker solutions. They may be disillusioned to find that the practitioner does not have the answers they hoped for.

A relationship built on safety, trust and mutual respect will be important as a foundation for working together.

Over time, the parent feels empowered to discover that they have some answers within themselves. They are healthy parents who can use their good parenting skills once they have a greater understanding of themselves and their children.

A DDP-INFORMED PARENT SUPPORT CONVERSATION

Rand is a single dad caring for his nephew, Ave. Ten-year-old Ave has lived with Rand since he was five years old. In the following dialogue, Rand is meeting with Marion, the DDP practitioner who supports him and Ave. This conversation follows a recent session with Ave when Marion noticed that Rand was struggling more than usual.

Marion: 'Lovely to see you, Rand. Sorry to bring you in from the garden on such a beautiful day.'

Rand: 'No problem, I just wanted to get some shrubs planted while it's dry.'

(*Rand and Marion chat about gardening for a few minutes as they settle into the conversation together.*)

Marion: 'I know how important gardening is for you. It can be really regulating, and I see you really need that just now. I received your text, so I know things are no better. Is Ave still struggling?'

Rand: 'Yes, he is. I'm not sure why. He just seems to wake up angry. I wouldn't mind if he talked to me, but all I get is insults and stuff.'

Marion: 'Rand, that sounds so tricky, and this has been going on for a while now, hasn't it? I see how much it is getting you down. I really see how this is eroding your confidence, and you have no one to tag team with. You're really getting the brunt of this.'

Rand: 'Yes, my sister tries to help, but she doesn't really understand. I think she still feels guilty because she didn't offer to take Rand, but that was five years ago. She had her young children to look after, I get that. Now, she can't understand why Ave behaves as he does. She thinks he should be grateful. I try to remind her of what he experienced, but she doesn't want to think about that. She was always close to our brother. His slide into alcoholism really hurt her.'

Marion: 'Caring for a sibling's child is complicated, isn't it? You all grew up together, and yet your experiences have been so different. I expect your sister wants to help but you are both holding lots of feelings, and she isn't having the day-to-day experience of Ave that you're having. Tell me about this week. I'm sorry it hasn't been any better.'

(*Rand talks about Ave. He has been holding it together at school but at home he is just full of anger. Rand is finding it increasingly difficult to stay patient and admits his worry that he could lose it with him.*)

Marion: 'Thanks for being honest, Rand. I see how hard this is for you. I'm not surprised you're feeling like this given what Ave is throwing at you. I'm not judging you for getting angry, although I see how much you're judging yourself. Let's focus on you. (*Rand grimaces.*) Yes, I know how uncomfortable you find this. Again, I'm asking you to trust me. I think this will help and we ran out of time last week, didn't we?'

Rand: 'Okay, I do trust you, really. I just find this so hard. It's like revealing the hardest things about myself. Not comfortable things.'

Marion: 'I know, we'll go slowly, and let me know if you need to stop. I really want us to think about the impact Ave's anger has on you. Obviously, no parent would find this easy. I'm wondering what you find the hardest though; those moments that you lose empathy and fear you will get angry back.'

Rand: 'It's those times when I start to feel afraid. When Ave raises his voice. He also has an expression on his face, a bit like my father used to have when he was angry with us.'

Marion: 'Oh, that's interesting. Ave reminds you of your father and then you start to feel afraid of him.'

Rand: 'Not of Ave, no, I'm not afraid of him. I'm afraid of me, what I might do. Of course, I don't want to get angry with Ave, but it goes deeper than that. At home, if we got angry, we would get hurt. I think that is part of it too. I'm afraid of getting angry because of what I might do but also what might be done to me. Does that make any sense?'

Marion: 'I think it does. It sounds to me as if there is an adult part of you wanting to protect Ave and a child part that is still locked in the past, those times when anger led to your father's punishment. Past and present are colliding here, aren't they? So, when you hear Ave's raised voice, or you see that expression on his face I guess it's hard to remember that this is a child in distress?'

Rand: 'Absolutely, and my instant response is to try and avoid it or shut it down.'

Marion: 'So, that's when you might move away?'

Rand: 'Well, I don't want to stay in case I do something I'll regret. But also, it just feels so hopeless. It just keeps going round and round and I can't change it, so I want to get away from him.'

Marion: 'So, there's a sense of hopelessness attached to the fear?'

Rand: 'I think so, both hopeless and helpless. Yes, and some of that is connected to when I start getting frustrated. I mustn't get angry. I've seen what that does. I've experienced what that does. I don't know what else to do but to put some distance between us.'

Marion: 'And your mother, what would she do, when feelings were raised in the family?'

Rand: 'I've no idea. I've no recollection of my mother ever supporting me or comforting me. She didn't get angry like Dad did. She just wasn't around. Well, I guess she must have been there, but I don't remember what she did.'

Marion: 'I see. Your dad was angry and your mum kind of wasn't around. Neither of them helped you with your feelings. So now, I'm wondering what happens to your anger when Ave is being challenging. Because you will be feeling it.'

Rand: 'I just squash it down. I'd rather pay for it internally than let it out.'

Marion: 'And what's the big fear of feeling angry?'

Rand: 'I've seen what anger does. I've seen the damage it does. It's very powerful for me.'

Marion: 'It sounds as if feeling any anger is hard for you. You've heard me say it before, feelings are just feelings, not right or wrong. As a child, you've seen one aspect of what damage anger can do. This makes it hard to hold on to there being some helpfulness in expressing anger sometimes. It's how you do it that counts. Ave is trying to figure that out, and it seems to me that you are too. I really get it; that fear is very real and very present. It's a fear from the past and it's really controlling you in the present. Ave doesn't know how to express his anger safely, and you're trying so hard not to feel it.'

Rand: 'I suppose my fear is that it's like a dam. If the dam bursts, we all get hurt.'

Marion: 'I get that. You never had experience growing up of anger being safe. There's a point when Ave is angry, where you notice your own anger. Then you experience fear and feel helpless and hopeless. So, you withdraw from Ave, a bit like your mum maybe. The alternative seems to be one where he or you get hurt. It seems to me that your past experience with anger is impacting on your parenting. Do you see what I mean?'

Rand: 'Yeah, I think so.'

Marion: 'I guess Ave is experiencing some hurt that's led to his behaviour. My guess is it would be hard to empathize with his distress when you're dealing with your own stuff. I see you're trying to make sure he's safe, but I wonder if this is stopping you doing other things that could help Ave.'

Rand: 'But isn't keeping him safe the most important thing?'

Marion: 'Yes, safety is. I suppose what we're discovering is that you're trying to keep Ave safe from a fear that is in your past. Maybe you can be angry, and still be present with him. Instead, you move away, and I wonder how Ave makes sense of that?'

Rand: 'I want him to be safe from what I experienced, and to some extent what he experienced with his father. I don't want him to ever experience that from me.'

Marion: 'Your motives are so good, Rand. Of course you want to protect Ave from violence. I think you're a long way from that though. Your father, and your brother, I guess they never learned how to regulate their strong feelings. I believe you can, but Ave doesn't see that if you withdraw from him when he's angry. For example, how is Ave learning how to manage his own feelings of anger?'

Rand: 'I guess I've never thought about it like that before. I do go back, once he's calm again. I try to talk to him, but he doesn't want to. I don't push it as I can see him getting riled again.'

Marion: 'Do you think he could be learning that expressing negative feelings is a bad thing? He doesn't know what else to do though. I wonder how that leaves him feeling.'

Rand: 'I see what you mean. If he feels as if he's messing up, no wonder he doesn't want to talk to me.'

Marion: 'And then there's a whole layer underneath Ave's anger. If he's getting the message that he mustn't feel anger, what happens to the distress, the worry or the anxiety? How does he learn how to manage that if you become unavailable to him at the point where he's feeling angry? You're doing that with good motivations because you want him to be safe. I wonder, though, about the unintended consequences.'

Rand: 'Gosh, it's complicated. I feel as if I've really messed up.'

Marion: 'I noticed that you started to look uncomfortable. I hope you're not feeling I'm judging you because that's certainly not my intention. You've been working so hard to give Ave a different life. I'm hoping, as we figure this out, we'll build on the good work you're doing with him.'

Rand: 'I don't really know what's wanted from me. It feels as if I'm not doing it right. That hurts, but if I can learn a different way to be there for Ave then I'll give it a go.'

Marion: 'It's tricky, isn't it, and my apologies, I certainly wasn't intending to judge you. I do think there's a consequence to this that is not helpful for Ave. I also recognize that you're having to deal with this every day. You're having to manage your own responses, to protect Ave and yourself from something you fear could be unleashed. I mean, that just feels enormous to me.'

Rand: 'But it's not something that I consciously consider.'

Marion: 'No, but unconsciously it's huge, having to live your life managing your feelings like this. We started today thinking about what happens when Ave gets angry and how tricky that is for you. In your younger years, there was no one to show you how to manage negative emotions like anger. Your mum didn't support you. She just kept out of the way, and your dad was abusive. Those were your templates, avoidance or violence. If anger isn't an option, all you're left with is avoidance. Now, as an adult, I'm suggesting you need to figure out how to manage these emotions differently. How is this sitting with you?'

Rand: 'I think I get it. I would like things to be different, put things in the past back into the past. I feel a bit hopeful that this could change things for Ave. I've been so busy trying not to get angry with him that I haven't stopped to wonder what might be going on for him.'

Marion: 'Let's have a think about that next time. We'll have a think about what's going on for Ave, and how to help you and him to manage angry feelings.'

Rand: 'That feels good. I think Ave and I will be figuring this out together. Perhaps I'll get him doing gardening with me!'

31

Your Presence Helps Me to Know How to Be Present With My Child

In this chapter, we explore the power of presence. I'm sure you have at some time been affected by the presence of someone. Notice how one person creates a sense of safety when another doesn't?

Can you see how a helpful presence can have a chain response? When we experience the positive presence of someone supporting us, we are more able to offer this presence to a person we are supporting.

Within DDP, we describe this presence as PACE. When we meet someone with this attitude, it sets the foundation for the relationship. A PACEful presence provides non-judgemental and non-blaming support.

Notice how PACE is being modelled within such relationships.

> 'When you model the model, I understand the way of being more deeply.'

When a model is being modelled, we understand it differently from just being taught about it. Think of trainings you have experienced when the trainer is either modelling or simply talking about a model.

REFLECTION MOMENT

Think about a work, parenting or caring situation.

★ What was modelled to you from those supporting you, and how did this impact on the person you were caring for or supporting?

Have you ever experienced this type of presence to be a bit too much?

Parents, just like any of us, can feel overwhelmed when feelings of vulnerability and even shame are evoked.

REFLECTION MOMENT

★ Can you think of an example where someone's presence was overwhelming and you were left in this state, and another where the overwhelm was supported?
★ What was the difference in the second approach that you found helpful?

It is important that the relationship is founded on trust and mutual respect. Within this there will be sufficient co-regulation between the pair to make the exploration manageable. The parent discovers that it is safe to be vulnerable. This leads to increased insight both about themselves and the child, and therefore more productive exploration of how to support the child.

Throughout, the parent is getting an embodied experience of PACE within the DDP model. They are experiencing it rather than just being told about it. This experience helps them to know how PACE can help them to be with their child differently, and this brings a richness to their parenting of the child.

> 'Modelling the model helps parents to adopt the model with their children.'

Consider understanding as providing a foundation.

Just like a house without foundations, the solutions will be much less stable and effective without understanding. The parent discovers how much richer support that leads to understanding is compared to a narrow focus on what to do. The latter does not explore the experience they are living with and therefore solutions are not supported by understanding.

THE POWER OF MODELLING

The manager comes into work at the residential home with a heavy heart. Waiting for the results of medical tests that have still not arrived, she feels a knot of anxiety inside. The knot tightened when her partner told her not to worry as they both left for work. Arriving at the residential home she sits down and spends a fruitless hour trying to make the budget fit the demands being made on it.

The deputy comes in. He's not interested in the challenges the manager is wrestling with. Instead, he wants to complain about one of the residential carers he's supervising who is still not managing the workload expected. The manager tells her deputy that she doesn't have time to think about it just now. He will just have to deal with it. The deputy feels his knot of anxiety tighten as he anticipates more disrespect from the residential carer, who always seems to brush his concerns away.

As anticipated, the supervision does not go well. The deputy clearly outlines the expectations of the residential carer, but this seems to fall on deaf ears. He protests that the expectations are unrealistic and there is a veiled threat of bringing in the union representative.

The residential carer walks into the living area feeling despondent. He doesn't know how he is going to fit in collecting one of the children when he has promised one of the boys, Charlie, some table tennis practice, and the incident report must be finished before the shift ends. The knot of anxiety is tightened by the worry that he could lose this job. With another child on the way he can't afford to be out of work. He grabs the car keys, calling out to Charlie that the table tennis practice will have to wait until tomorrow. As he drives back his head is full of the incident and how he is going to record it. The child, feeling ignored, slumps sullenly in the car. The rest of the shift is a tense one, with the children all arguing and fighting.

The report doesn't get written.

The manager goes home fretting about a budget that still isn't balanced.

The deputy spends the evening trying to figure out employment law and what options he has for managing the residential carer.

And the residential carer? It's a tense evening as he takes over making the tea and getting his three-year-old to bed while his partner gets the bed rest the doctor has ordered. He knows his resentment is impacting on his partner and child, but not being able to finish the report weighs heavily.

None of them sleep well that night.

A new day comes, with the same worries.

The manager comes downstairs and looks hopefully for a letter. Her partner shakes her head and commiserates with the long wait. Handing her a cup of tea the partner starts to say: 'Don't worry,' and then stops herself.

'Of course, you're worrying,' she says. 'I feel hopeful given the statistics we were told but that's no help to you. I get that. Waiting for that letter must be agonizing. I imagine you can't hope given the worst that could be facing you. With budgets and statistics, I bet you could scream at numbers just now!'

The manager laughs, 'You've got that about right. Still, the sleepless night wasn't totally wasted. I think I've figured out what I could do with the budget.' Giving her partner a kiss on the cheek she sets off for work.

Once at work, the manager pushes the budget to one side and calls the deputy in. 'I'm sorry, I know I didn't help yesterday, and I see it was a difficult night with the children. Do you want to go through it now?'

'And I wasn't very supportive with your budget worries,' says the deputy. 'Let's both sit down and see if we can help each other.' For the next hour the two of them work together, exploring the plans for the budget and thinking about how they could support the residential carer. As they are talking, they realize how much they have lost their curiosity. They were so keen to make sure the residential carer conformed to their expectations they hadn't stopped to wonder what might be making things hard for him. They agree to slow down and explore this before considering any action they might take.

In talking to the residential carer, the deputy learns of the difficulties his colleague is facing. His partner's high blood pressure means she might need to go into hospital. The carer is taking on a lot of the household responsibilities, including meeting the needs of their young child. The deputy begins to appreciate how much the carer is managing and to feel respect for the way he is balancing this with his job.

In addition, they think about how good the carer is in engaging the children while the challenges he has with attention deficit hyperactivity disorder (ADHD) and dyslexia are contributing to difficulties with paperwork and organization. They agree that they will come up with a support plan to help him in the areas he is struggling with, while ensuring that they all benefit from his strengths with the children.

The carer returns to the children with a much-reduced knot of anxiety. Charlie looks at him hopefully.

'Yes buddy, we'll get that table tennis practice in tonight. We need a plan, and you can help me with it.'

They fetch pens and paper.

'Now let's think, Joe needs help with his maths homework; that should take half an hour. I need 15 minutes writing up some notes and then we can have 45 minutes playing table tennis.'

'And don't forget tea,' says Charlie. 'We've got to eat as well.'

'Good thinking. It's a good job I've got you to help me. Ah, I see you've fitted it in while I'm writing my notes. That should work, as Aleck is around to help as well.'

The evening goes smoothly. The children are settled, and they all sleep well that night.

DDP-INFORMED PARENTING SUPPORT

Part 5

DDP IN THERAPY

We have been exploring DDP as an approach for practice and parenting, with PACE as the attitude at the heart of this. In this final part, we consider where it all began: DDP as a therapy for children, supported by parents.

Have you come across myths about therapy? It is not the quick fix that is often envisaged. There are no magic wands that make the impact of trauma go away, although I understand why we would wish there were. Therapy is hard emotional work, which takes time and energy.

REFLECTION MOMENT
Think about what therapy means to you.

★ What do you expect from therapy?

I view therapy as something that helps children develop emotional resilience to the impact of trauma.

Dan Hughes, when developing DDP, was searching for an approach for children who had experienced abuse and neglect. The children were living within foster care or adoptive homes, and he recognized the need to help them restore their trust in being parented. With sufficient safety and security, they could begin to heal from the effects of their early experience.

Since those early days DDP has grown and developed for children who have experienced relational traumas wherever they are now living. This has been informed by:

• *attachment theory* – helping us to offer safety to the child

- *intersubjectivity* – providing the child with relationships that are reciprocal in that each is open to the influence of the other. This in turn supports the child to explore the world
- *neuroscience* – providing environments that facilitate healthy brain development.

The DDP model has expanded in ways that provide support for the child's:

- *emotional well-being* – through healthy relationships and therapy
- *behaviour* – through DDP-informed parenting
- *learning* – through education staff who are DDP-informed
- *development* – through family and community environments that meet the child's needs.

Can you see how therapy is a part of helping a child recover from poor early experience? It is a therapy model, within a parenting model within a practice model.

In this final part, we explore DDP as therapy.

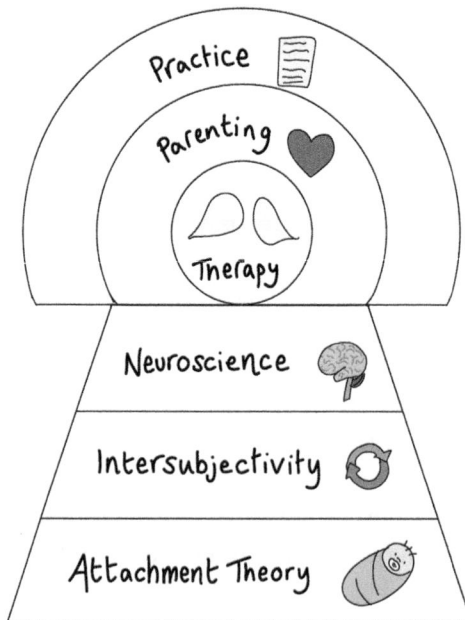

32

Only When You Feel Safe Will Healing Happen

As with any part of the DDP model, we begin in safety.

Safety is the bedrock of therapy, as it is of home and school life.

I wonder where your attention would be focused if therapy were not a safe space. Could you imagine making progress without safety?

> 'I offer you safety and ensure that we return to this place when it is lost.'

Without safety, we cannot expect progress. This also means that we must not rush therapy. Allowing time to go at the child's pace, finding and returning to safety and leaving space for fun and relaxation are all part of the process.

Within DDP, one of the main aims of therapy is to help children to explore the trauma that they have experienced. For children experiencing separations from their birth family and other caregivers, this includes mourning losses.

> **REFLECTION MOMENT**
> Think about children who have experienced trauma and loss. Remember how this shows itself in relationships, behaviour and day-to-day function.
>
> ★ What would you like to be different for them?

I expect health and happiness are high on your list, maybe alongside behaviour changes!

When caring for these children, it is understandable that we want the therapy work to happen sooner rather than later. We all want children to be happy and well adjusted, with good emotional and physical health. We do need to have realistic expectations.

Therapy for traumatized children:

- is rarely a quick process. The DDP model suggests a longer-term view of supporting the child
- needs to account for their relationship experience. It makes sense to involve safe caregivers in the child's therapy. The DDP model supports the view that what has been harmed within caregiving relationships also needs to be healed within safe caregiving relationships. We want children to seek and enjoy relationships
- is supported by the environments they are experiencing. As mentioned in the introduction to this section, if home, community and school relationships are DDP-informed, the children will be living in safe and healing environments that can support therapy.

REFLECTION MOMENT

Think about a child you are supporting in therapy.

★ What signs do they show that they are not safe?

★ What do you do to build safety for them?

In previous books I have written about a pyramid of need. Perhaps you have seen it. I developed this many years ago to help people understand why we don't always move as quickly as they would like to bring children into the therapy room.

Therapy is best viewed as a long-term rather than a short-term process which is supported by the day-to-day experience of the child and always rests on helping the child to feel safe.

The pyramid illustrates how the *exploration of trauma*, including mourning losses, is most helpful when the children have some experience of:

- *physical and emotional safety:* relationally traumatized children often feel very unsafe in the world, so restoring a sense of safety is a priority

- *relationships as a source of safety:* relationally traumatized children will often avoid or try to control relationships, therefore avoiding reciprocity. Only when relationships feel safe will children be open to their influence

- *being able to accept comfort and co-regulation:* when children are afraid of the influence of the other, they are not able to accept comfort or the support that will help them regulate emotionally and behaviourally. Children need to feel safe accepting comfort and co-regulation

- *having empathy for self and others:* this rests on the ability to reflect on experience. Children develop empathy and reflectivity within their early relationships. The child impacted by relational traumas often does not have this experience. Children need to feel safe with others so that they can develop empathy and reflection from within these relationships.

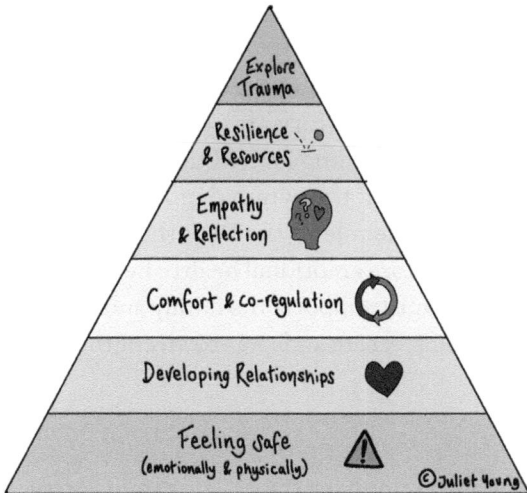

All of these will *build resilience and develop emotional resources*. Without resilience and resources such as capacities for regulation and reflection, children will continue to struggle. This in turn impacts on how they view themselves. Often, they perceive themselves as a bad child who does not deserve love and support.

As the child experiences safety in their relationships, they are revising their sense of who they are – a child who is loveable and worth supporting. This in turn develops increased self-esteem, which strengthens their emotional resilience. These support the child in therapy while the therapy process itself strengthens all parts of the pyramid.

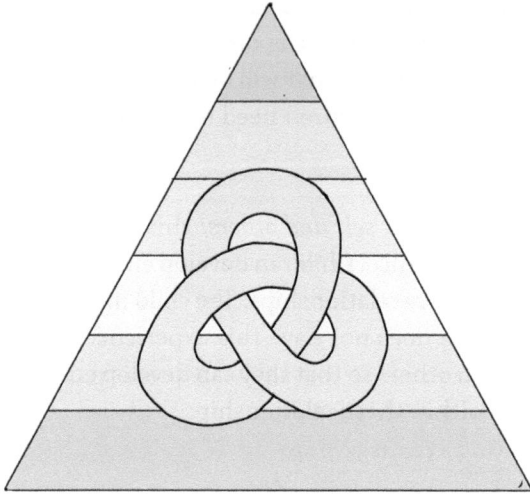

While I have illustrated this as a pyramid, it is not a linear process. Rather, it is a backwards and forwards experience. Are you familiar with the image of a never-ending knot? I think of the pyramid of need as a bit like this, each part of the pyramid influencing every other part.

I hope you see how the role of the DDP therapist is not just about exploring trauma to restore emotional health. Before, during and often after therapy, the therapist supports the family and other close relationships to help the child feel safe and thus to strengthen all the elements of the pyramid.

'The DDP therapist prioritizes the child's safety above everything else. When the child is feeling safe, other work can happen.'

HOW CAN I TRUST IN THE SAFETY YOU OFFER?

Safety means...
Warm arms that feel like a blanket wrapped
around me, holding me close.
Looking into your eyes and feeling the love and gentleness there.
Knowing that when I walk out into the world you are watching me.
The smells of my favourite foods being prepared in the kitchen.
When I mess up, your kind discipline helping to make it right again.
When I fall and am hurt, your gentle arms catching and soothing me.
And when I go to bed, you tuck me in tight and
tell me stories that lull me to sleep.

This was not my safety before you and so...
I push the blanket of your arms away, knowing that they will hurt.
I avoid your eyes fearing the hate and harshness that will be there.
I go into the world looking for danger that I'm sure will come.
I distrust the smells you make, and so reject the food I'm offered.
I mess up over and over, sure that this time you will leave me.
I fall, I jump up, I fight back. I hide hurts so you miss my pain.
And when I go to bed, I lie awake watching
and listening for what is coming.

The therapist...
Wraps me in a warm blanket while you hear the story of my fears.
Talks with a quiet voice while telling me what they see in your kind eyes.
Holds my hand while I look around the space and see the safety there.
Fills the room with the drinking chocolate smells that we all enjoy.
Knows when I mess up and helps me to hear when you say you will stay.
Helps me to trust in your gentle hands when I fall and when I hurt.
And then, when I go to bed we remember the safety
that we have brought home with us.

And little by little I learn to trust in the safety that is around me now.

33

I Help You to Relax Into Our Connection Each Time We Meet

Can you see how safety and connection are intertwined?

The way we connect impacts on how safe or threatened we feel. It is in relationships that we feel our most safe or experience most psychological danger.

REFLECTION MOMENT

★ How does a child you are supporting cope when they meet other people, whether familiar or strange to them?

Children impacted by relational traumas work hard to reduce the sense of danger in any meeting with people.

They may avoid this meeting, evading any interest the other shows in them.

They may be over friendly, trying to please the other with their chatter and their forced smiles.

The beginning of a therapy session is therefore an important moment. The therapist ensures that they are ready to greet the child, knowing that any preoccupation they take to this meeting will be met with suspicion. At this initial connection, at the beginning of each session, the child needs to experience themselves as important to the therapist, that they have their full interest. They need to feel that they do not need to work to make themselves safe.

This is the importance of 'connect and chat'.

The therapist meets the child with interest and delight. They discover what is of interest to the child and demonstrate that they too are interested in this. The child discovers that the therapist wants to know about the whole of them. They are not just concerned with their behaviour, their trauma or their successes and failures. They want to know the child because the child is worth knowing.

> 'When I connect and chat, you know the whole of you is of interest to me.'

This is why the DDP therapist begins with 'connect and chat'. If the child leads with a worry or concern, the therapist will follow this. Often the child prefers a gentler start, with time to discover together an interest of the child's, a nice experience they have had recently or something they are currently enjoying.

'Connect and chat' helps to establish the intersubjective connection between the child and therapist around safe themes. Remember, intersubjective means an emotional connection within which the child feels safe to be open to the influence of the other. These intersubjective connections are important when exploring harder themes. It helps the child be open to exploring their current and past experience, even when this experience is difficult for them to think about.

As the therapist and child explore intersubjectively, the therapist is discovering the story of the child's experience.

We talk a lot about stories within DDP. Discovering stories, retelling stories and witnessing stories. These are not fictional stories, although these too can be a part of therapy. Mostly they are narratives of experience. As the child experiences their story being heard, retold and witnessed, they discover this story in a new way. This in turn changes the way the child experiences themselves.

During 'connect and chat', the child experiences stories being discovered about their current interests and excitements.

> 'Through connect and chat the child experiences their interests through the eyes of another.'

This is a gentle exploration without the challenge of experiences that the child fears or is troubled by. This sets a storytelling tone and rhythm for the whole session.

The therapist and child then move backwards and forwards between gentler moments of exploration of lighter themes and interests and exploration of the more difficult themes which are more challenging. The therapist follows a pace and rhythm that suits the child.

A therapy session contains moments of:
- *connection and chat* about current interests and joys
- *connection and exploration* of the themes that are more troublesome and challenging
- *connection and relaxation* in moments of fun and calmness.

The parents are included in this as well. The therapist leads, while inviting the parents to support and witness the work that the therapist and child are doing together.

REFLECTION MOMENT

Think about a time you have spent with a child. How much time did you spend:

★ connecting and chatting
★ connecting and exploring
★ connecting and relaxing?

Do you think you got the balance right between these three activities?

'Connect and chat' plays an important part in helping the child to feel safe enough to move into those areas where trauma has impacted. It is the exploration and witnessing of these areas that will allow healing and emotional growth to occur.

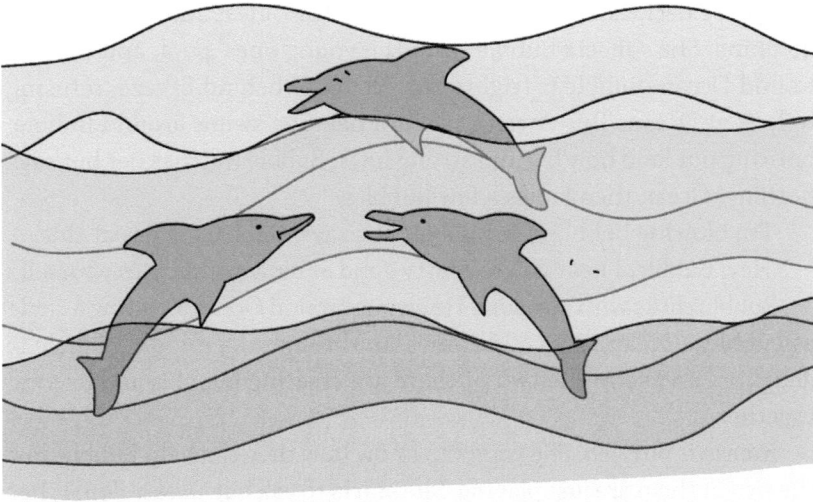

THE DOLPHINS' DILEMMA

The pod of bottlenose dolphins is struggling. They live off the coast of Scotland, and the local fishing trade has been causing difficulties. The noise from the marine traffic is interfering with their ability to communicate with each other, to navigate and to hunt for food.

Recently, a female dolphin died, orphaning her young calf. She was trapped in one of the driftnets. The pod spent hours holding her up, valiantly trying to save her, but their efforts were in vain.

Maybe it is time for the pod to move. There is an area further around the coast away from human interference. They could move there, but it will mean navigating through a dangerous area of water. For several months they have debated whether they should stay or go. It is the death of one of the pod that makes their mind up. The danger of the journey is less than the fear of more accidents while sharing space with the fishing community. They will go.

They are worried about the orphaned calf, Bubble. He is still very small, and he is missing his mum. One of the other dolphins, Breeze, has taken over caring for him but he isn't doing well. He has stopped playing and is constantly looking for his mother. He is young to make the journey, and he doesn't want to go without her.

Breeze decides to consult with one of the oldest and wisest of the dolphins. She collects Bubble from the young ones' pool, and they go to find Ocean. Bubble is frightened. He hides behind Breeze, refusing to look at Ocean. This doesn't concern her. She swims around Bubble, noticing out loud how big and strong he is. Bubble watches her but says nothing. Ocean then blows a few bubbles.

'I'm blowing bubbles for Bubble,' she says. Bubble giggles at this.

'Hey, Bubble, I hear you're pretty good at blowing bubbles yourself.'

Bubble clicks with pleasure. He swims around Ocean, creating a circle of bubbles. Ocean dives and comes up through the middle. Bubble is delighted and soon the two of them are creating bubbles and leaping together.

Breeze is puzzled. She wants to know how they can help Bubble, but the two of them are just playing. She starts to ask but Ocean signals her to stay quiet. Instead, she invites Breeze to play with them.

They have been playing for about 20 minutes when Bubble pauses and looks sad. He looks at Ocean and says: 'My mum said I'm good at blowing bubbles because that's my name.'

Ocean knows it is time. Bubble is ready to talk.

'You miss her a lot, don't you?' she says.

Bubble's whistles and squeaks say it all. He tells Ocean that he has looked everywhere but cannot find her. Bubble swims between Breeze and Ocean while they explain to him that his mother has died and cannot be with them any more. The pod now has to move on. They have to find somewhere safe where they can play, hunt and swim.

Bubble frowns. 'Mummy told me we mustn't swim over there. There is bad water that I mustn't swim in.'

'Your mummy was right,' says Ocean. 'A young calf must not swim there alone, but you won't be alone. Breeze will be with you, and we'll make sure that other adults are close by.'

'Will we find mummy on the other side?' asks Bubble.

'No, I'm afraid not,' says Breeze. 'But I think that your mummy would be happy that I'm looking after you. I'll stay right by your side for the whole trip.'

Bubble clicks his pleasure at this idea. 'Can Ocean swim on the other side of me?' he asks.

They agree that Breeze will swim on one side and Ocean on the other. They will keep Bubble safe through the dangerous water.

'Will I feel less sad where we're going?' Bubble asks.

'No, I think you'll feel sad for a long time,' says Ocean, 'but Breeze and I will be with you. Let us know when you're feeling sad, and we'll stay close by. I think your mummy would be very proud of her champion bubble maker who is going on such a hard journey.'

You will be pleased to hear that the pod safely navigates the dangerous water and finds their new home. Away from the fishing boats and other marine traffic they settle in well. Bubble still feels sad at times, but he also enjoys playing and soon there are more calves to play with. Breeze, supported by Ocean, looks after him until he is old enough to start a pod of his own.

Bubble grows up to be a fine adult dolphin. He is as wise as Ocean, and guess what? His mother chose his name well. He is always the best bubble maker of them all.

34

PACE Is My Guide to Offer You Safe Connection

As you have noticed, PACE has been a thread throughout this book as it is through all DDP approaches. PACE is an integral part of all therapy sessions.

> 'PACE helps us to view our children differently.'

PACE is also a way of being that helps us to be kind to ourselves and to support each other. Therapist, parent and child are all bathed in PACE, supporting the therapy work.

REFLECTION MOMENT

★ Can you think of times where elements of PACE have helped you to feel more emotionally connected with someone?
★ Did you notice any changes to the way you viewed the other person as the emotional connection strengthened?

Therapy helps the parents to view their child differently.

A parent might be feeling frustrated with their child. It is hard to be PACEful when it feels that our child is being deliberately difficult. In a therapy session, the therapist, with more emotional distance, can be empathic and curious.

'That sounds hard when... I wonder why...'

As the answer is discovered, empathy and acceptance increase and the parent can enjoy their child again.

Let's dive into an example to help us understand this more deeply.

I want you to imagine that a parent, Helen, has called the therapist ahead of the child's next session. She and her partner, Gail, have had a difficult weekend with their adopted daughter, Elisha, getting cross over the tiniest thing. She has fought with her brother, refused to eat her meals and has been getting up several times a night, coming into her parents' room to complain of noises, smells, sounds. 'It's as if she wants to wear me out,' Helen tells the therapist.

The session begins as usual with Elisha and her therapist settling into their routine. Elisha usually brings something to show her, and today has a painting from school. After some 'connect and chat' they look at the painting together.

It's a picture of the family. In the middle are Helen and Gail standing together with Elisha's brother, while Elisha is at the edge of the painting. Helen appears to be holding something in her arms. The therapist is curious about this, but Elisha is distracted and becoming dysregulated.

The therapist brings in some regulating games, which end with Elisha sitting between Helen and Gail while they have a drink and a snack. The therapist wonders again about the picture. Calm now, Elisha tells the therapist in a matter-of-fact voice that Helen is holding her new baby. 'It's a girl,' she says. 'So, they won't need me any more.'

REFLECTION MOMENT

★ Can you figure out what has happened?

It takes them a while to untangle it, with lots of empathy and acceptance for how hard it is to worry that your mother is going to have a baby and how frightening to think you won't be wanted any more.

After a few more distractions Elisha tearfully tells them that she overheard Helen on the phone. She heard her say that she was excited that it was going to be a girl, as she had always wanted a girl of her own.

Overheard conversations can lead to muddles, and Elisha is hyper-vigilant to what Helen is doing. The conversation was with a friend of Helen's who was pregnant with her third. Having two boys, the friend was excited to be having a girl!

Helen and Gail hug Elisha to them. Following the therapist's cue they stay with empathy for how scared Elisha must have been, and then they explain the muddle and let Elisha know that neither Helen nor Gail is having a baby.

Smiling now, Elisha says, 'I'm going to make another painting. Can I have my paints when we get home?'

'Of course,' says Helen.

'Maybe we can make a family painting together,' Gail suggests.

Can you see how the therapist is PACEful in a way that is difficult for the parents in the heat of parenting? With the therapist's help, the parents witness their child's story unfolding and their PACE increases. The therapist holds PACE for all of them and this resolves the muddles that can arise, especially with an insecure, hypervigilant child.

'PACE is the attitude which helps me to connect with you and your experience.'

We will meet Elisha again and see how the therapist builds on this work in future sessions to further deepen understanding of Elisha's experience, in the light of her traumatic history.

WHEN PARENTING JUST FEELS LIKE A FAILURE

The therapist sits with the parents in their despair. Another frustrating week with Taylor. More trouble in school and total disrespect at home. They don't know how long they can keep going.

The therapist must decide if it's safe to bring Taylor into the session. This time with the parents will be important.

'I see you're at the end of your tether,' says the therapist. 'I know this isn't what you want. It's so hard and so different from the dream you had when you adopted Taylor. I wonder what the hardest part is, right now. The part that makes you feel as if you can't go on.'

The parents consider this. The school difficulties are worrying, but they do have good support from the teachers. Taylor's angry outbursts can be intense, but they know that these will pass. What they really struggle with is the disrespect. They were both brought up to respect their parents. Taylor's disrespect makes them feel as if they're failing him.

The therapist responds, 'That does make sense to me. Respect is an important value and signals your success in raising a child. No wonder this is the part of parenting Taylor that leads to despair. How do you make sense of this disrespect?'

The parents answer this question by focusing on their failure. The therapist is accepting and empathic. Space is given for the parents to feel fully listened to. Gently they then move on to reflecting on Taylor.

What has been his experience of respect growing up? In what way does his disrespect help him to feel in control? What does safety feel like for Taylor?

As they talk about this, the parents remember the years Taylor was at home with a father who disrespected everyone. They remember the two foster placements with carers who found Taylor to be too challenging, and the one placement where he experienced some stability but then had to move to be adopted by them at the age of seven.

'It makes sense that Taylor doesn't know how to respect us,' says one of the parents. 'Why would he even want to respect us? What respect has he ever experienced? Perhaps we've been expecting too much. Maybe success is just about hanging in there until he feels safe enough to trust us.'

The therapist smiles and playfully says, 'It looks as if you're getting the hang of this parenting stuff.' Then more seriously, 'I think we're ready to bring Taylor in, don't you?'

Taylor's session goes well. The parents watch as the therapist responds PACEfully to Taylor's distractions and to his communications that life sucks and he doesn't want to be adopted any more. As the therapist sits with curiosity, Taylor becomes more vulnerable. He admits that he's feeling frightened all the time.

'Any idea what you're frightened of?' asks the therapist.

'I'm just waiting to be moved again,' he admits. 'I'd like to stay but I can't help getting cross.' He looks at his parents. 'I would like to stay, but why would you want me?'

The parents' frustrations melt away as they look at their son. Empathy and acceptance come easily to them now as they hold their frightened boy. 'We want you to stay too. We'll just have to keep working at it. After all, who else will get the cat to take her medicine!'

They all laugh and just in that moment they feel successful as parents and son.

35

How Can I Adopt PACE When It Is Different From Everything I Know About Parenting?

Before we leave this exploration of PACE in therapy, let's think about how PACE can fit in with different cultures.

As part of the preparation for bringing a child into therapy, the therapist works with the parents. One of the things that they want to ensure is that the parents will also hold an attitude of PACE. As part of this work, the cultural background of the parents needs to be understood.

> **REFLECTION MOMENT**
> Think about the culture that had most influence on you as you were growing up.
>
> ★ Was this a culture that reflected your heritage, a culture that you needed to fit in with, or a bit of both?
> ★ What do you notice about the values you grew up with? How important were respect, achievement, family loyalty?
> ★ What were the views on wealth and health? How important and how wide was community in your upbringing?

When bringing PACE into parenting it is important to understand this experience. PACE needs to fit with cultural values, even if we ask parents to stretch away from their culture.

Culture

Trauma also comes into this picture. In Part 4, we explored how the child's trauma can impact within a family, and the additional impact of parental traumatic experience. This becomes even more complicated when parents are impacted by transgenerational trauma caused by oppression, marginalization and discrimination, which can be recent and historic. Culture and trauma can become intertwined and complicated.

Resmaa Menakem[1] draws a distinction between these. He notes how trauma can remain while the context has been lost:

> Unhealed trauma acts like a rock thrown into a pond; it causes ripples that move outward, affecting many other bodies over time. After months or years, unhealed trauma can appear to become part of someone's personality. Over even longer periods of time, as it is passed on and gets compounded through other bodies in a household, it can become a family norm. And if it gets transmitted and compounded through multiple families and generations, it can start to look like culture.

'When the impact of trauma becomes habitual, we can mistake it for culture.'

Can you see how this impacts on how parents adopt an attitude of PACE? The experience of a child's trauma, the parents' current or historic trauma and the culture they inhabit need to be understood and considered within a family.

---

1   Menakem, R. (2021) *My Grandmother's Hands*. London: Penguin Books, p.39.

Here are some thoughts I have had. You may have different thoughts. This is an area which needs continuing exploration.

I like to think that children across cultures are loved and valued, and that unconditional acceptance is a part of PACE that feels comfortable throughout the world. I also recognize that trauma can interfere with this, reducing acceptance and impacting on the parents' capacity to be PACEful. For example, a traumatized child can develop a range of challenging behaviours as a consequence of the impact of the trauma. If these behaviours lead a parent to feel a sense of failure, they experience less joy in the relationship, their curiosity about the child's experience underlying the behaviours reduces, and acceptance and empathy are lower. This is increased when parents hold their own trauma. For example, when the experience of colonization leads to the breaking up of families and the loss of children, parents with this history will be much more anxious about potentially losing their child, and this will impact on their way of being with the child.

When parents are well supported and less impacted by the child's or their own trauma then the attitude of PACE will be easier to hold and will be expressed more easily in authentic and culturally sensitive ways.

Let's explore these cultural differences a bit more.

Consider empathy: in talking with others, I notice how expressions of loving and valuing vary from implicit expressions via actions (*You know I love you because I lovingly prepare food for you*) to more explicit communications of love. This can impact on the way empathy is expressed, which may be through actions or words depending on what feels most natural.

Turning to curiosity, some cultures encourage overt expressions of curiosity about the internal world of another, especially when autonomy and independence are valued. The parents are interested in what the child thinks and how they make sense of the world. Raising children to be independent is a marker of success as a parent. In other cultures, when self is understood as part of community, the child's internal world is less of a focus. The child in connection with others is of greater importance, and the showing of respect to elders is valued, reflecting on the whole family. Curiosity about the child's experience is lower because instruction in how to behave is such an important part of being a successful parent.

Finally, enjoying and playing with children varies between cultures.

Parents connect with their children depending on the experiences they want their children to have. In some cultures, parents gain enjoyment in the relationship through playing with their children. In others, play with peers is encouraged while valued parent-child time involves the child in family tasks.

Can you see how PACE is an attitude that all parents can hold? Understanding the complex interaction between culture and trauma is important when supporting parents to discover and retain their authentic attitude of PACE.

REFLECTION MOMENT

Here are some questions that might help you to deepen your reflections about the culture you are familiar with.

★ What positive values did this culture give to parenting and to DDP practice?
★ Are there any negative values, perhaps impacted by historic trauma?
★ How can parenting and practice consider current trauma that children face outside the family because of their heritage?
★ How might PACE be adapted to take these considerations into account?

Maybe these questions are difficult to answer. On reflection, I notice that I hold an assumption that we all understand our cultural heritage.

Some of you may be thinking, but what if we don't have this knowledge?

A colleague helped me to understand how identities, culture and heritage can be stripped away through colonization, enslavement and the need to adapt to the Western culture that the family now live in. Ancestral histories and experiences are lost in the process. 'Who am I' becomes a complex question which can be determined by a need to be who others want them to be in order to fit in. Trauma continues and the need to survive is paramount.

DDP therapists encourage parents to bring PACE into their parenting while being careful to ensure that this is culturally sensitive. I'm beginning to understand what a complex process this is. We must start with building safety, while recognizing that this is a long process when working with families where safety is not their lived experience.

My hope is that over time therapist and parents can work together to figure out what is comfortable in parenting, both from what they know of their own heritage and from what DDP can offer. Parents can discover aspects of PACE that fit with who they are and want to be, and areas that they would like to adopt even though they feel more unusual to them.

> 'We'll figure out together how PACE fits for you. I will respect your values, and you will discover where you can stretch into new ways of being.'

Whether practitioner or parent, we all need to understand our own heritage and how this impacts on the way we adopt the attitude of PACE. We raise our children in line with the values we treasure while stretching into new ways of being undreamt of by our ancestors. In understanding ourselves, we are also better placed to help others to adopt this attitude in a way that is comfortable for them.

A JEWISH TALE: A PERSONAL REFLECTION

This story begins with Alexander and Sarah, my great grandparents. Alexander (known as Alec) was born in 1866 and Sarah two years later. They lived in a Jewish community in Volpa, Grodna, then part of the Russian Empire. They were two children among many growing up during the pogroms and witnessing the persecution of Jewish people. They married in 1884 under a chuppah, the marriage canopy. The matchmaker chose well, Alec and Sarah needed to be a strong couple to face what was ahead of them.

Two years later, the couple faced a difficult decision. The persecution and massacre of Jews was making life increasingly unsafe for them. Should they stay and see friends and neighbours killed or go and establish themselves in a foreign country, hoping that here would be some measure of safety? These were challenging choices. Alec and Sarah chose to leave the community, as many others were doing. They journeyed to London, England with their small son, Simon. They left behind everything they knew, including their parents, Udal Woolf and Annie, my great, great grandparents.

Udal and Annie are just shadows in this story as I know little about them. I imagine it was hard for them to watch their children go. They were unable to support Alec and Sarah in bringing up a large family in a foreign country. For a culture that loves family and tradition, it must have been especially hard to only know their grandchildren from afar.

And so, this story takes us to a family separated by discrimination and persecution. The threat of being driven from home and country was ever present. Alec and Sarah needed to learn a new language and establish a tailoring business, while raising seven children, including my grandfather, Jacob. They lived in a Jewish community in the East End of London. It was a relief in 1906 when Alec received his naturalization certificate, supported by Spitalfields Naturalization Society. They had some measure of security at last.

Alec and Sarah brought with them their Jewish heritage. They had absorbed the culture of the Shtetl they were raised in, influenced by their parents and more distant ancestors. Having left family behind, they valued the home they established and the family they raised. Alec was well respected in the community and became a master tailor. He had strong values around education and achievement, which were passed down to his children, many of whom followed him into the tailoring business, including my grandfather, Jacob.

Jacob was born in London around 1901 and married Deborah in 1925, the same year that Alec died at 59 years of age. Sarah lived on supported by her surviving children until 1940.

Jacob and Deborah had four boys, including my father, who grew up with a strong bond between them and an interest in achieving and accumulating wealth. The terror of having to flee from a country was never far away, and wealth provided some measure of security.

Wealth was certainly in my father Peter's mind when he chose careers for my sister and me. I was to go to university to study dentistry like my uncle, who was respected in the family for his education and the money he earned. You will notice that I rebelled!

Jewish families have strong patriarchs. The men are the spiritual heads of the family and have a role in choosing their children's future, as I mention above. Women are important. I wonder if Alec ever began a Sabbath meal by singing the *Eshet Chayil* to Sarah (translated as 'woman of valour', it extols the virtues of women). I witnessed a strong matriarchy in Deborah, my grandmother, who was formidable! My father also told us tales of Sarah his bubbe (grandmother).

Jewish children were told what they should think or feel and who they should marry. Deborah dearly wanted her boys to marry 'nice Jewish girls'. It strikes me how much a need for control runs through these ways of being. I'm sure being in control was important when so much control had been taken away.

Times were changing, however, and my father and two of his brothers married outside the faith. The Jewish community was beginning to break down as the Goldings increasingly assimilated into English society and raised dual heritage children.

And so, I enter the story. A third-generation child with Jewish and Yorkshire heritage being raised in England. I wonder what has been passed down to me through the generations. What ancestral trauma rests within me? What cultural values have I absorbed? Understanding how this has impacted me is important for me as a parent and a DDP practitioner.

Playfulness, acceptance, curiosity and empathy will all be impacted by our ancestral inheritance.

Reflecting on my Jewish roots, I can see how curiosity can be diminished when parents have a strong need to guide their children, safeguarding them by telling them what to do and think. The priority is a good education and learning a trade.

There is room for playfulness though, when children are precious, and family ties are important.

But what room is there for the apparent softness of acceptance and empathy when children need to be strong to survive?

And within a culture so impacted by loss and relocation, stories are important. They store the memories and keep traditions alive. The Goldings are skilled storytellers and stories were always there in my childhood, although curiously few stories of the impact of trauma or life in Russia were passed down. Maybe some things are too painful to be remembered.

As I reflect on this, I can see the values that helped me to embed PACE into my parenting and my DDP practice.

I value an upbringing that developed my playful and storytelling side. I think this also helped me to stretch into deeper curiosity.

I want to hold on to the importance of guiding children while also developing my acceptance and empathy.

I want to give children strength while recognizing that this can be combined with compassion.

I recognize I have a controlling side, possibly one of the scars of the transgenerational trauma I have inherited. I work at letting some of this control go to find room for increased acceptance and empathy.

I think about Alec and Sarah making that journey to find a safer world. I reflect on the thread that connects me to them via two further generations who lived through hardship, war and the horror of the holocaust.

I am the sum of all of this. PACE allows me to take the best from my heritage as well as to discover new, different ways of being that were not possible for my ancestors.

Alec and Sarah, early 1900s

36

Only in Co-Regulation Can We Truly Co-Create

We have explored the importance of safety, relationship and PACEful emotional connection within the DDP model. Can you see how these provide a foundation for all DDP approaches, including therapy?

The DDP therapist builds on this foundation to provide support for the child and family that facilitates healing from the impact of relational trauma.

REFLECTION MOMENT
Imagine building on this foundation.

★ What bricks do you think the DDP therapist needs to put into place?

The therapist helps the child and parents to discover the trauma stories that the child holds. In discovering these stories, new stories emerge. The trauma does not go away, the child's experience will always be with them, but now instead of stories of shame and terror the child holds stories of connection, strength and resilience.

'DDP therapy is a process which aims to transform trauma into healing.'

To achieve this, the therapist facilitates co-creation; the therapist, parents and child together discover the narratives of the child's current and past experience. The child needs to be in a regulated state to engage with this.

Can you see the next layer the therapist provides?

Co-regulation is an important part of therapy sessions, which is essential for the co-creation we will explore next.

Regulation has been mentioned a few times in this book. Let's slow down and think about what this means.

REFLECTION MOMENT

★ What is your relationship with your emotions like?
★ Do you experience moments of peace and contentment?
★ Do you get excited when anticipating something you are looking forward to?
★ Do you experience love for those close to you? And do you manage feelings of anger, frustration or sadness?

You will recognize all these feeling states – they are part of being human.

How well we deal with our emotions will differ from person to person. I wonder if you have experienced times when your emotions overwhelm you. I expect you have, and it is not a pleasant experience. We describe this as dysregulation because it becomes hard to regulate our emotional states at these times.

Maybe you have also noticed feeling shut off from your emotions, which is equally unpleasant. Do you recognize a feeling of being frozen, or distant or perhaps a sense of deadness? This also suggests emotions that are not regulated but instead of dysregulation this is described as dissociation.

REFLECTION MOMENT

★ Remember times when you felt dysregulated and co-regulation from another helped.

We are at our best when our emotions are in a state of balance. Dan Siegel[1] describes this as an integrated state and likens it to a river with a bank on each side. On one bank is the chaos of dysregulation and on the other is the rigidity of dissociation. When we are flowing in the river we are in a regulated state.

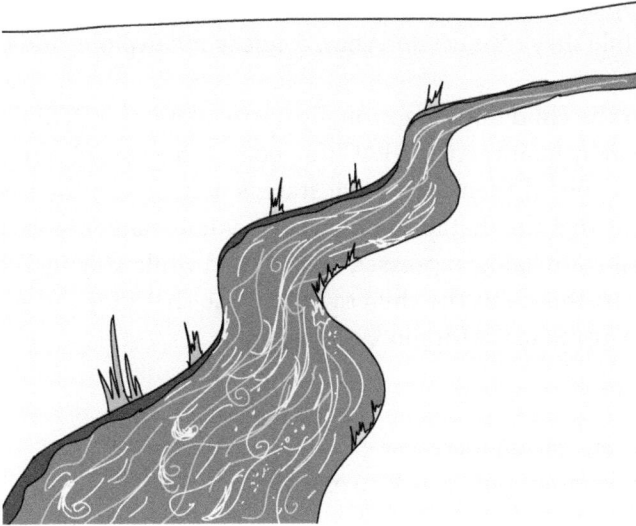

Siegel also uses the analogy of a window of tolerance. Within our window we are regulated, when we move above the window, we are dysregulated, and beneath it is dissociation.

Which metaphor do you prefer? I personally like the image of a river best.

Guess where a child needs to be emotionally if they are going to engage with their stories?

Yes, within their window of tolerance, flowing gently along the river.

Children are born unable to regulate their emotions. An infant is reliant on a parent to regulate for them. A young child is beginning to learn how to manage their emotions but remains reliant on their parent to co-regulate with them.

Without this early parental influence, a child will develop weak

1   Siegel, D.J. (2010) *The Mindful Therapist. A Clinician's Guide to Mindsight and Neural Integration.* New York: W.W. Norton & Co.

regulation skills. This is what we commonly find with children who have experienced relational traumas.

When we relate this to therapy, and the exploration of experiences that the child finds challenging, we can understand the importance of the adults providing co-regulation for the child. The adults' presence, touch and words help, alongside food, drink and regulating activities. The therapist's aim is to help the child to stay in their window of tolerance while they connect and chat, connect and explore, and connect and relax.

When the child does emotionally dysregulate, the DDP therapist helps them by maintaining a PACEful, open and engaged stance. Children are helped if their emotional state is matched by the therapist. This means that the therapist matches the vitality and intensity of the emotional state being expressed by the child while staying regulated themselves. This helps the child to regulate so that they can engage in reflection again, ready for more co-creation.

- Co-regulation increases emotional balance.
- Co-creation puts words to experience.

'My presence holds you steady when you wobble. Through my co-regulation, you join me in co-creating your story.'

A STORY OF DYSREGULATION AND CO-REGULATION

I once witnessed a man become dysregulated during a train journey. He was responded to differently by two members of the railway staff. This incident has inspired this fictional story of dysregulation and co-regulation.

Ethan is taking his regular Friday evening train journey to visit his mother. These weekend visits are bitter-sweet. An only child, he is close to his mother, but her gradual deterioration caused by dementia is hard to see. He wants to be a supportive son, but at times he feels frustrated with her increasing confusion.

To help his mother, Ethan follows the same routine each week. Just before boarding the train, he talks to her on the dementia-friendly tablet he has given her. He lets her know when he will be arriving.

He has 20 minutes left of his journey when they pull into his mother's local city. Ethan puts away the report he's been working on. He enjoys this last part of the ride travelling through the countryside of his childhood. He is pulled back in time as they pass familiar landmarks.

It is, therefore, with some consternation that Ethan hears the announcement made by the train conductor. The train will be terminating at the station. Passengers are advised to disembark and wait for the next local train to continue their journey.

Ethan can feel anger rising. All his careful preparation with his mother is in disarray. She will be even more confused by his late arrival. It is going to be a difficult evening. As he steps from the train, he recalls other train journeys disrupted for a variety of what seem like spurious reasons. Leaves on the track, the wrong kind of snow, high winds bringing down power lines. Why couldn't they design a rail network that could cope with English weather!

Ethan's anger spills over as he marches to the station master's office. He bangs on the door, exclaiming loudly that this is not good enough. Why can't they run the trains properly? He needs to be somewhere important, and their inefficiency is making life impossible for him.

As he rants the door slowly opens. The station master emerges, a little red in the face. It is quickly obvious that he too is enraged. He loudly tells Ethan that he cannot be responsible for the difficulties on the train lines. Ethan needs to be patient like everybody else. The local train will arrive shortly. Ethan is not calmed and continues to argue.

On and on it goes. Ethan's anger is matched by the station master who will not be verbally abused in this way. The other passengers quietly step back as they watch this altercation.

Luckily the local train arrived, or who knows how this would have ended. Ethan boards it, still fuming. He sits in his seat unable to enjoy the passing rural scenes while he continues to ruminate at the injustice of a train that can't keep to a scheduled timetable. When the train conductor passes through the carriage, Ethan has another target. He begins his rant again.

The conductor pauses and listens for a moment. Looking at Ethan, he slowly puts his hands on his hips. With intensity and energy that matches Ethan's emotional state, the conductor exclaims, 'You're quite right. This isn't good enough. You deserve a rail service that gets you where you want to go on time.'

Ethan opens his mouth ready to have another go, but he can't find the words. Like a balloon deflating, his anger has dissipated. The conductor looks sympathetically at him and asks, 'Where are you heading, mate? It seems as if it's important to you.'

Ethan, feeling soothed, tells the conductor of his mother's difficulties and the importance of predictability for her. The conductor listens quietly before saying, 'We don't know what stories our passengers are living through. You all deserve the train service you need. I'm sorry we've let you down.'

'It's not your fault,' says Ethan. 'You're not responsible for the difficulties on the train lines.'

The rest of the journey is uneventful. Ethan calls his mother's neighbour who agrees to let her know that he has been delayed. She stays with her until Ethan arrives, calm and ready to spend the night with his mother. They have a happy evening looking through some old family photographs.

As Ethan goes to bed, he recalls the kindness of the train conductor and even feels a little sorry for the station master who had felt the full force of his frustration.

37

Follow-Lead-Follow Offers a Rhythm to Our Exploration

Safety, connect and chat, PACE and co-regulation. The pieces are in place to discover the child's story and to help a new story to emerge.

We all make stories of our experience. Can you recall doing this? Maybe a close friend has failed to be in touch. You reflect on the last time you met and remember that you had a disagreement. The story you tell yourself is that the friend is hurt, and this is why you have not heard from them. You may even feel irritated that this friend is so sensitive to a small difference of opinion.

This is your story, making sense of a current experience in the context of a past experience. Then you meet up with a mutual friend and hear about some difficulties the friend is having. In a moment your story transforms.

Within DDP therapy, the therapist helps the child to experience their stories being heard with acceptance and empathy. This is the child's experience in that moment. The therapist follows and witnesses the story. The next step is to lead the child into some further co-creation, making sense of the story in the context of current and past experiences. Out of this exploration a new story emerges, transforming the child's experience of themselves and others.

Within the DDP model we call this process *follow-lead-follow*. The follow helps the child to be heard. The lead helps the child to explore their experience more deeply.

This is not just a search for facts and information. The therapist explores the affective experience of the child in relation to these. The therapist is facilitating an *affective-reflective dialogue*.

As with any good storyteller, the therapist tells this story to the child and parents, attending to both content and experience.

Content is what happened. This is the reflective part of the story.

Experience describes the expression of the emotion associated with this content. This is the affective part of the story.

'The affective-reflective rhythm to the storytelling allows the full experience of the story to emerge.'

Bringing affect and reflect together leads to a story with more depth and impact. It helps the child to feel deeply understood.

Notice how the therapist is both non-directive and directive within this joint discovery. As the therapist follows the child, they move into themes that are important and of interest to the child. The therapist then becomes gently directive, leading the child into a deeper exploration of the theme.

REFLECTION MOMENT

★ Which is easier for you – to follow or lead?
★ Can you think of times when you have combined these two as you chat to someone?

Do you remember Elisha, whom we met in Chapter 34? You will recall that an overheard conversation led Elisha to think that one of her adoptive mums was pregnant. The muddle needed correcting. The therapist, supported by Helen and Gail, heard Elisha's story with acceptance and empathy and then untangled the muddle by helping Elisha to understand what she had overheard.

This follow-lead-follow stayed in the present. The adults understood Elisha's story of a new baby and then co-created a new story of a friend's baby.

There was a part of Elisha's story that was left unexplored during this session. Can you spot what it was?

Recall that Elisha described how, in her painting, Helen was holding her new baby. This is the part of the story that the therapist followed. Elisha then said: 'It's a girl, so they won't need me any more.' This is a theme that also needs following. An opportunity arises a few sessions later.

Elisha is excited to tell the therapist that they went to visit the friend and her newborn baby girl. The therapist is interested in all the details that Elisha wants to relate, while looking for an opportunity to lead Elisha into some deeper exploration. It's important to explore Elisha's fears that there could be a time when she's not needed any more. The therapist needs to be patient, waiting for the right moment when Elisha will be open to this.

Follow-lead-follow is an important part of helping Elisha experience this worrying story of fear and anticipated loss.

This is how the session develops.

Follow: Elisha talks about the baby and how she was allowed to hold her very carefully.

Lead: The therapist notices that Elisha was good at holding the baby carefully and wonders how she knew how to do this.

Follow: Elisha remembers she often held her brother when he was a baby, especially when her mother was asleep on the sofa.

Lead: The therapist remarks on what a helpful big sister she was and wonders about this big responsibility when she was only little herself.

Follow: Elisha talks about how she tried to look after her brother, offering him toys and food when he was crying. She is tearful remembering her mummy being cross when he didn't stop crying, and then how she and her brother went to the foster home.

Lead: The therapist reflects how scary this must have been and how much they must have missed mummy. The therapist wonders how Elisha made sense of this.

Follow: Elisha snuggles into Helen as she tells the therapist that it was her fault they had to leave. She didn't look after her brother very well and her mummy was cross.

Lead: The therapist is sad that Elisha had such a difficult time trying to look after her brother and then thinking it was her fault that they were moved to foster care. The therapist then notices how little Elisha was. Too little to take care of her infant brother. The therapist then has a big idea.

'Oh my gosh, I wonder if you were scared that this would happen again, if Helen had a baby. You wouldn't be able to look after the baby and then they would want you to go! No wonder you get frightened when Helen or Gail is cross with you. No wonder you worry that they might not need you any more.'

Looking at Helen and Gail, the therapist then suggests to Elisha that they tell this story to them. While they have been listening, retelling the story deepens the experience for Elisha. It helps her to be open to Helen and Gail's empathy and acceptance for how worried she gets that she isn't good enough for them.

Follow-lead-follow has helped Elisha to have a fuller understanding of her experience with Helen and Gail, and all the worries that she holds. As Elisha is led more deeply into her story, she experiences her feelings being understood.

Retelling the story to Helen and Gail helps Elisha to experience their acceptance and empathy. They understand that she experiences herself as not good enough, and they don't want to send her away. They do want her to understand her mother's story and why she went into foster care, and they hope that one day Elisha will know that she is a good girl, who, like all children, can sometimes get things wrong.

Elisha's sense of self shifts a little as she experiences the love, acceptance and empathy that surrounds her.

Follow-lead-follow develops an affective-reflective dialogue which brings the heart into connection with the mind. This co-creates a rich story within which the inner life of the child is explored, deepened, elaborated on and made more coherent. The story that emerges touches and changes the experience of those witnessing it, including that of the child.

> 'I follow where you lead and lead you to where you need to go.'

ROWAN'S GUIDED JOURNEY

It is a big day for Rowan. One she doesn't feel ready for, but she's put it off twice already and the elders are getting restless. Three tree years have passed since they first suggested she was ready for her guided journey to become a novice. The elders insist that she delay no further. Time has run out.

She has known this day would come, and she has always been afraid. Always there has been a small voice inside her head telling her she will fail. She will lose her place in the community.

It doesn't matter that no one has ever failed a guided journey.

It doesn't matter that all tree elves have to go on this journey.

It doesn't matter that this is the journey that will direct her path as a novice.

Rowan knows she will fail. She knows the journey will end with abandonment by the only community she has ever known. She will have to survive in the world alone. She is not worthy, just as the day of her beginning had revealed.

But time has run out and so Rowan steps away from the tree that she calls home and meets her journey guide, Beech.

Beech takes her to the path of discovery, a little way out from the community. Rowan has never visited this place but somehow she feels at home here. She walks lightly among the leaf litter, careful not to disturb any creatures who dwell there. She enjoys the soothing feeling of the gentle breeze on her face. And then she remembers why she is here. A spike of anxiety rises within her and the gentle breeze becomes a gale. Beech holds her steady as the wind buffets her.

'Look at me, Rowan,' he says. 'I'm with you. We'll do this together.'

As Rowan calms, the gale becomes a breeze once more. She looks at Beech waiting to be told what to do.

'This is your journey, Rowan. You lead and I'll follow,' he tells her.

Rowan feels a pull towards a path veering to the left. She follows this, and they walk into a part of woodland that feels old and strong. She walks along noticing the tallness of the trees, feeling their self-sufficiency. These trees are confident or so it feels. She stops and looks around. In front of her are two trees that are entwined with each other. Where their branches touched, they make an arch.

'Good,' says Beech. 'Here's your first Treeway. Take my hand. I'll lead you through.'

Rowan feels a strange reluctance to move forward, but she does what she is bid. Beech holds her confidently and they walk forward.

'What do you see?' Beech asks.

Rowan sees herself asleep in a branch of the tree she recognizes as home. One of the novices sits near her. The novice looks up, and to Rowan's surprise speaks to her.

'You were too strong and independent,' they say. 'Why was that? I wanted to be your friend, but you never let me in.'

Rowan reflects on this. Is she independent? Her anxiety tells her otherwise. She tries hard not to need anyone but inside she is waiting to be found out. She isn't strong, not really. She just tries to look as if she is.

'I see you,' Beech whispers. 'You were so frightened all the time. You worked so hard not to need the others. I figure it was pretty lonely for you.'

Rowan feels a tear roll down her cheek. She never cries. Where has this come from? She is lonely. She never feels as if she fits in. She never believes anyone wants to be her friend. She recognizes the novice now. It is Elm. They were tree mates, partnered up for lessons before Elm moved on. Had they really wanted to be her friend? How had she not noticed?

'You're not alone now,' says Beech. 'Let's figure out what you were frightened of.'

And so, the journey continues. Rowan leads the way, following a path only she can feel. Each time they come to a Treeway, Beech leads them through. They discover together what is there.

In this way, Rowan finds her younger self – a child of about nine or ten tree years. She is so busy running around. Willow, the caregiving elf who looks after the orphaned elves, stands nearby. She turns to Rowan.

'I was trying to look after you but all you wanted to do was look after me. Look at you, doing one job after another. You never let me care for you. You never played with the other elflings. Why did you always try so hard?'

Rowan remembers how exhausting it was. 'I needed to please everyone,' she tells Beech.

'What would happen if you didn't?' asks Beech.

'I don't know,' Rowan replies. 'They'd be cross with me, I guess. I couldn't bear it when they were disappointed in me.'

'You were frightened of displeasing Willow and the other caregivers,' observes Beech. 'I see that. You worked so hard that you forgot to play. How sad you must have felt.'

Rowan feels the sadness within her as they walk back to the path. She leads them to the next Treeway.

Rowan is now a toddler being cared for by Willow. Rowan watches her young self as she follows Willow around. She's forgotten how bossy she was. She wanted everything her way. She told Willow what to do, what she would wear, what she wanted to eat and where they should go. Willow looks back as the toddler pulls her away.

'It was exhausting,' she said to the older Rowan. 'You knew your own mind, that's for sure. I wanted to take care of you, but it was hard. I'm sorry I got cross and frustrated with you.'

Rowan has forgotten. Willow was so kind, but did get cross too.

'It wasn't your fault,' she tells Willow. 'I was awful to you.'

'You were doing what you needed to do, that's all,' says Willow. 'I just wanted to take care of you, but I couldn't find my way in.'

'I was bossy,' Rowan tells Beech.

'I see that,' Beech muses. 'But you were so little, and I think you felt out of control. Things were happening to you, and I guess being bossy was the only way to feel safe. I wonder why you felt so out of control?'

At the next Treeway, Rowan feels more reluctant than ever. She doesn't want to follow Beech through. They stop for some refreshments. Rowan wonders about the younger selves she has met and why they behaved as they did. She feels so much loss inside her. Loss of a caregiver who could help her. Loss of play and playmates. Loss of friends and being able to rely on others.

'Why did I lose so much?' she asks Beech.

Beech takes her hand and leads her towards the Treeway. 'I think it's time to find out,' he says.

Despite her reluctance, Rowan follows Beech through. She is facing a Rowan tree. She can see a bundle among the branches and the shadowy figure of an elf leaving. Rowan watches with horror and then turns away.

'Come on,' says Beech. 'Let's look together.'

Rowan holds tight to Beech's hand as they approach the bundle. Beech gently lifts it down and unwraps the cloth. Rowan takes one look and recoils with horror.

'It's horrible,' she says. 'Please take it away.'

'I see a tiny infant elf,' says Beech. 'Take my hand and have another look.'

Rowan does as suggested, and is surprised to see what Beech has seen. Not the monster of her first imagining, but a tiny, helpless infant.

'It's me, isn't it?' she says. 'This is where I was left.' Rowan reaches out and takes the infant from Beech. She cradles it in her arms as Beech talks softly.

'She's so tiny and helpless, just waiting for someone to care for her.'

'Why did she abandon me?' asks Rowan.

'I don't know, Rowan. Your mother must have been desperate. Maybe we'll never know why.'

'I thought it was me,' Rowan speaks thoughtfully. 'All these years I believed that it was something that my mother had seen. Some badness in me that made her get rid of me. But look, I was just a tiny infant elf. How could I have been bad?'

Then Beech talks softly to Rowan of all they have seen on their journey. He starts where they have ended, with the little foundling elf waiting for someone to care for her. He talks about how hard it was for this little one to accept care when she understood her beginnings. How fear of what was inside her led her to reject the care and friendship she was offered. She thought she needed to be bossy. She thought she needed to please. She thought she needed to be independent.

'What you really needed has been right there waiting for you,' he comments.

'What do I do now?' Rowan asks Beech.

'We go home to the community,' answers Beech. 'There you'll find what you've been missing. You'll have time to play. You'll have time for friendship. You'll be cared for. In time you'll find your purpose and you will be ready. Maybe you'll even be a journey guide like me.'

Rowan smiles. 'I thought this guided journey would lead to more abandonment, but instead you tell me I could be a guide like you! My head is spinning.'

Beech smiles back. 'Your future is waiting for you, but there's no rush, Rowan. You have some catching up to do first.'

38

You Speak to Me With Your Words and Your Actions

I wonder if the following questions have been in your mind as we've been exploring the co-creation of a story.

- How can you co-create a story with a child who says very little?
- Are you not just telling the child what they think and feel?
- What if the child doesn't want their story discovered?

These are all questions I am asked during training. They are valid questions and deserve careful thought.

In answering these questions, we need to think about communication. How do we communicate with others what has happened and how we think and feel about it? What do we choose to tell, and what to hide? How does this vary depending on the person we are talking to?

REFLECTION MOMENT
Think about how you communicate with people.

★ If you have a worry or fear, who do you choose to talk to?
★ How do you choose what to say and what to keep to yourself?
★ Do you have friends or family members who seem to know when you are not talking about something? How do you think they know?

When you thought about this, I expect that you were aware that you don't only communicate in words? Some of our communication is non-verbal and our verbal and non-verbal communication don't always match. While we can shut down our words, hiding body language is harder.

The child who says very little can be saying a lot. The therapist listens to these non-verbal communications as well as the words the child is offering. Together these inform how the story develops between them.

REFLECTION MOMENT

★ What body language do you have that is used for communication? How do you 'speak' with your eyes, your hands, your legs, your shoulders?

★ Do you notice other people responding to these non-verbal communications?

The therapist listens carefully to all communication. As the therapist pays attention to the child's body language as well as their words, therapist and child are creating the story together.

It is important that the therapist also pays attention to their own wishes and feelings about the child. It can be easy to slip into the story something the therapist would like the child to think or feel. This moves them away from co-creation and is not helpful. By monitoring themselves, the therapist can notice and have empathy for their wish to make the child feel better through offering them some wise words and thoughts. They can then return to noticing what the child is actually communicating.

Notice the difference between:
- 'Your mummy has lots of struggles. She does love you though. Maybe it's hard for you to imagine that when she doesn't turn up, but you know it's hard for her to get to the meeting.'

And

- 'You recognize that your mummy struggles, and it feels as if she doesn't love you. You know that your mummy doesn't love you; thanks for correcting me. I get that. How could you believe she loves you when she doesn't turn up to see you?'

Follow-lead-follow, as explored in the last chapter, is dependent on following the child's verbal and non-verbal communication. The therapist decides when to follow and when to lead.

The child might communicate, 'I don't want to talk about this.' Sometimes the therapist follows this and moves the conversation to lighter themes. Sometimes they gently lead the child on. This decision is often based on understanding what the child's body language is communicating:

- 'I can't do this just now. It's too overwhelming. I don't want to feel this vulnerable.'

Or

- 'I want you to know this. I'm just not sure I can trust you. Will you be able to handle my vulnerability when we talk about this?'

The therapist responds differently to these communications. Of course, they sometimes get it wrong. Reading body language can be tricky. This is when relationship repair is needed, which we will explore in the next chapter.

> 'All communication is non-verbal, and some communication is also verbal.'

When the verbal does not match the non-verbal, the discrepancy often reveals hidden fears and worries. Noticing these discrepancies helps the therapist to understand the experience of the child.

'You're telling me you don't care. I get that. It's less painful not to care. I'm wondering though, I notice how tense your shoulders are right now, and that right hand is looking as if it really cares. I'm guessing you really don't want to care. It's so hard to care, isn't it? Your big sigh as I say this makes me think that maybe I'm right?'

Noticing and talking about the discrepancy allows the therapist to co-regulate the child's experience more helpfully. This can create a space where it feels safe for the child to continue. When verbal and non-verbal match, the communication will be deeper and more open, and the story creation more helpful.

'I notice your verbal and non-verbal communications. Discrepancies between these help us discover your fears and worries.'

THE BOY WHO IS FINE

Fourteen-year-old Jesse and his therapist are talking about losing his mum to a world of drugs and alcohol. He had cared for her when he was too little; now he doesn't even get to see her. The only verbal response the therapist gets is that it is all fine. Jesse's body tells a different story.

Here is how their conversation goes:

Therapist: 'How is it fine? I can only guess at the worries you might have, not being able to see her.'

Jesse's words: 'No point worrying. I'm fine here and the social worker will let me know if she's not okay.'

Jesse's body: Jesse holds himself very still and tense. His right hand starts to drum on the seat, matching some slight tapping of his left leg.

Therapist: 'I get that worrying doesn't change anything. It's kind of hard not to worry though, and I can see that in your legs. I wonder if you're trying hard not to worry?'

Jesse's words: 'Maybe, I have to work at it, but really, I'm fine. I have exams coming up. I want to focus on those.'

Jesse's body: There is more tension in Jesse's body as he puts his hand on his leg to stop it tapping.

Therapist: 'Wow, that feels a lot. Not seeing your mum and exams. Help me understand how you're managing this.'

Jesse's words: 'I'm fine. I keep saying the same thing. I don't know what else to say.'

Jesse's body: Jesse breaks eye contact to look out of the window. As he does so he leans closer into his foster carer. She can feel his body shaking.

Therapist: 'I can see how tough this is. Yes, you keep telling me you're fine and I'm glad you're comfortable living here. It's a lot to manage though, and I see your body working very hard to manage it. I wonder how it would feel to let us help you. I'm guessing that isn't something you're used to.'

Jesse's words: 'How could I be used to it? I've always managed on my own. It's what I do. I'm not sure I know any other way.'

Jesse's body: As he talks, Jesse's body relaxes a little. His head rests on his foster carer's shoulder just for a moment. He then sits up straight again.

Therapist: 'Yes, how could you know any other way? You've always had to manage. You took care of your mum. You made sure your brother had breakfast and got to school. You went to school and pretended everything was all right. You worked so hard to keep the family together. I really respect everything you did. I also feel sad that there was no one taking care of you through this.'

Jesse's words: 'It was fine. Well okay, it wasn't fine, and I failed in the end didn't I, because here we are?'

Jesse's body: The agitation in Jesse's words can also be seen in his body. He gets up and paces around the room.

Therapist: (*matching the intensity that Jesse is now showing*). 'Yes, that's true. You tried so hard to look after your mum and to keep the family together, but in the end, you couldn't do it. It must hurt so much trying to do something that no young child should have to do (*lowering his voice, with less intensity*) and I can only imagine how worried you must be not knowing how your mum is.'

Jesse's words: (*also with less intensity*) 'I am worried. The social worker promised to tell me, but we haven't heard anything. What else can I do but carry on?'

Jesse's body: As Jesse talks, he moves back to the sofa and sits next to the carer again. She reaches out an arm and he sinks into a hug with her. 'I'm here,' she says. 'I can't change anything, but I'm here.' Jesse looks at her and smiles as his body relaxes further.

Therapist: 'It's been so hard for you. I'm glad you've been able to share this with us today. And look at that body of yours, it surely knows how to be supported. Thank you for trusting us to help. I know that it hasn't been easy.'

39

I Will Be Vigilant for Signs of Rupture, Offering the Repair Needed

Would you agree with me about the importance of a parent helping their infant to stay in, or return to, a regulated state?

The parent attends to physical and emotional needs and in this way the infant can tolerate any emotion they are feeling without becoming overwhelmed.

Have you heard advice that attending to a crying baby spoils them? What people giving this advice fail to understand is that an infant cannot regulate these emotions themselves and is therefore reliant on a parent for this.

A large part of this regulation comes from the presence of the parent. The emotional connection the parent has with the infant is central to their regulation. For this reason, the parent is attentive to this connection, noticing when it becomes disrupted and then making sure to restore the connection again.

This is known as relationship repair.

Ed Tronick[1] has recorded many hours of parent-infant interactions, slowing these down to track the rupture-repair cycle.

I remember seeing one of these recordings. A mother is changing her infant. The infant reaches out and grasps a handful of the mother's hair. The mother frees her hair and then comforts the now crying infant.

It is only when the recording is slowed down that you get a fuller

---

1   Tronick, E. (2007) *The Neurobehavioural and Social-Emotional Development of Infants and Children.* New York: W.W. Norton. & Co.

picture. At the point the infant grabs the hair you see an instinctive display of anger on the mother's face as she experiences pain. This is so momentary it was not noticeable at the normal speed. The infant is aware of it, though, and cries in their distress. The attentive mother quickly soothes the baby.

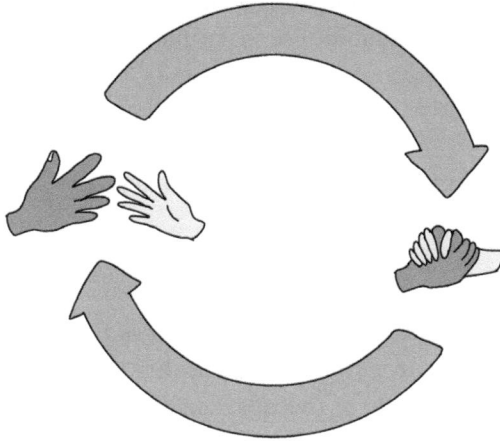

REFLECTION MOMENT

★ Can you recall experiences of ruptures in a relationship? Consider small ruptures as well as more significant events.
★ Notice the many reasons that relationships rupture.
★ How easy is it to repair when a relationship ruptures? Can you think what gets in the way?

These rupture-repair cycles are a normal part of human relationships. In Ed Tronick's work with infants he estimated that the child and parent are only emotionally synchronized for 30% of the time.

Reassuringly he also lets us know that the rupture-repair cycles are important for the development of regulation and learning to manage difficulties and conflict. The critical part for the emotional health of the child is that the parent works to repair the relationship when the ruptures occur.

Ruptures are a natural consequence of living together, of sharing social relationships. Think of a repair as a way of saying: 'My relationship with you is important. You matter to me and therefore I'll work to bring us back into emotional connection again.'

Rupture and repair provide a rhythm to relationships. For a child, it is important that the adult attends to this rhythm. The adult is responsible for repairing the relationship, whether this follows a need for discipline, a time of unavailability or just when attending to the normal ups and downs of a day.

> 'In my attention to rupture and repair, you discover your importance to me.'

Within the therapy relationship, it also follows that it is the therapist who attends to ruptures that arise. The therapist always attends to even the smallest rupture in the relationship and ensures that this is repaired before continuing.

When adults are vigilant for relationship ruptures and take responsibility for repairing these, it demonstrates to the child that they are important and the adult views the relationship as precious.

ATTUNEMENT IN A SILENT WORLD

Naomi is pregnant at 16. Her parents aren't thrilled about it. Out of work and out of options, bringing a new baby into the home feels like a burden too many. However, they want to stand by Naomi. They rejig the small three-bedroom house, putting the three boys into the biggest bedroom and fitting out the tiny box room with a single bed and a cot.

The pregnancy is uneventful in the early stages, although Naomi isn't great at looking after herself. She often misses appointments with the midwife. Later she develops high blood pressure and is advised to rest. Naomi resents this. She sneaks out to meet her friends, eager to show off her 'bump'. In the end, Naomi is admitted to hospital so she can be monitored. Baby Eva is born at 32 weeks, a small fretful baby. She remains in the special care baby unit for the next three weeks, providing an opportunity for the nurses to help Naomi learn to look after her.

Coming home is stressful. Eva is frequently unsettled, and Naomi struggles to soothe her. Her mother tries to help, but a crying newborn in what is already a busy household is challenging. Naomi frequently puts Eva into the second-hand pram loaned to her by a friend of her mother's. The motion of the pram soothes Eva to sleep, and Naomi enjoys showing her off to her friends. Despite all their cooing over her, Eva sleeps soundly at these times.

The health visitor is worried. Naomi is often out when she visits, and she can see the stress building in the family. Eva is missing important developmental checks. When she does get to see her, the health visitor notices Eva's slow growth and fretfulness. She also has reddening of the ears. Eva has missed her newborn hearing test, but the health visitor notes that she doesn't startle to loud noises. She watches Naomi with Eva. It is not a comfortable relationship. Eva does not settle easily, and Naomi often misses cues that Eva needs soothing. A referral is made for social work support.

With the social worker's support in place, Naomi attends a rearranged hearing test for Eva. As the health visitor expected, this reveals that Eva has severe hearing loss.

More tests are needed to understand the extent of loss and to consider options. Eva might be suitable for a cochlear implant, and the medical team want to trial a hearing aid as part of the assessment. It will also give Eva needed exposure to language.

The social worker is reluctant to consider this until Eva's home life is more settled. Naomi is already finding the medical appointments stressful and is anxious about introducing the hearing aid. The social worker can also see that a deaf baby is one stress more than Naomi's parents can manage despite their commitment to Naomi and Eva.

However, no one wants Eva to miss out on what she needs in these critical early months.

The social worker sits down with Naomi and her parents. They discuss what they all need and agree together that the best option is to find a mother and baby foster placement for Naomi and Eva.

Sometimes in life the pieces fall into place. Lila and Jordan are newly approved foster carers able to offer a suitable placement. In addition, as a Deaf family who have raised their own child with hearing loss, Lila and Jordan are ideally placed to support Naomi in caring for Eva. They are also close enough that Naomi's family can remain involved, and Naomi will not lose touch with school or friends.

Naomi settles in well. She enjoys the extra space and is happier to spend more time at home. Lila and Jordan start to teach her sign language which Naomi picks up quickly.

Most importantly, Lila and Jordan are on hand to help Naomi with her relationship with Eva. They can see how unsettled the two are. Eva signals distress or discomfort, but Naomi either misses it or does not have ways to soothe the infant. However, when Eva is settled and sleepy, Naomi chooses these times to try to play with her baby.

Naomi is young and inexperienced, and the pair are in a state of misattunement most of the time –a smooth rupture/repair cycle needs to be established.

Lila and Jordan also help Naomi to understand the silent world Eva is existing in. They show her ways to soothe Eva with touch and sight. They help Naomi to know when Eva is ready to play, and guide her in the ways of playing that are most suitable for a deaf baby.

With Lila and Jordan's support, Naomi learns what her daughter needs, and feels more confident introducing a hearing aid. The world does not need to stay silent for Eva.

With the move from misattunement to attunement, Naomi becomes a more confident mother. She enjoys visits from family and friends and feels important as she teaches them how to sign as well.

Naomi becomes so attentive to her baby that Lila and Jordan have to remind her to go out. It is okay to fit in some normal 16-year-old friend time as well!

40

Witnessing Another's Story Is the Greatest Privilege a Therapist Has

I have talked a lot about the co-creation of stories in previous chapters. I have mentioned witnessing these stories but only in passing. Join me now to explore witnessing in more depth.

First let's remind ourselves of why stories are important within the DDP model.

> ...our childhoods leave in us...stories we never found a way to voice because no one helped us to find the words. When we cannot find a way of telling our story, our story tells us, we dream these stories, we develop symptoms, or we find ourselves acting in ways we don't understand.[1]

Humans are born storytellers and the story is a universal form of expression. Stories in one form or another are found in all cultures. It therefore makes sense that an ancient practice of storytelling should find its way into therapy.

The use of therapeutic stories and storytelling relies on finding the story for the person engaged in therapy. It is the narrative of their experience that the therapist seeks. The story is discovered in the safety of the relationship between therapist and child.

When relationships are safe and connected the story will appear.

---

1   Grosz, S. (2013) *The Examined Life*. London: Chatto & Windus, p.10.

REFLECTION MOMENT

★ When you think of the word 'story' what comes to mind?

Often when we think of the word 'story', we think of fictional stories. Fiction is one way of describing experience, and fictional stories can be incorporated into therapy sessions.

Have you had experience of a child responding to a story in a way that reveals their fears and worries?

I remember working with a child and reading a simple story of a dog who kept being naughty despite his best attempts to please his owners. As the child listened, he commented that the owners would get rid of the dog now.

Sometimes this non-direct way of communicating fears and worries is all a child can manage.

More directly, the DDP therapist can help the child to tell their story. Some people prefer the word 'narrative' to story as it moves them away from the concept of the story being fictional. Whether 'narrative' or 'story', we are helping the child to voice their experience.

Therapist and child explore the child's story together, discovering the themes that colour the child's life. These stories are sometimes playful, often serious, and always compassionate. This is an act of discovery of the child's experience. By doing this with safety and openness, the child's feelings of shame or fear associated with their experience become smaller. New stories emerge from this joint exploration.

In this way, the child's life story becomes integrated rather than fragmented and their sense of self more positive and coherent. This helps them to develop resilience to the impact of the relational traumas they have experienced.

Let's turn our attention to the act of witnessing someone's story.

REFLECTION MOMENT
Consider why you tell friends or family members about experiences you have had.

★ How does it feel to have your story witnessed?

> ★ What do you find most helpful when they respond to your story?

Storytelling and witnessing go hand in hand.

> 'Therapist as storyteller is also witness.'

The therapist is not the only witness in the room during a DDP session. As therapist and child discover the story, the parents are also witnessing it.

And then, when the therapist retells the story that has been discovered, the child too becomes a witness.

Why do you think it is important for the parent to witness their child's stories?

The child experiences vulnerability as their fears, worries and doubts are discovered. This vulnerability stems from fears of not being good enough, not acceptable to their parents. The child therefore becomes anxious about what will happen next. The fear of abandonment is never far away for children who have experienced relational traumas and loss of parents. The therapist helps the child to discover that their story has been heard and they are still acceptable to their parents.

This involves a retelling of the co-created story. The therapist helps the child to tell their parents the story. The child knows they have been listening, and yet this retelling deepens the experience of this. In hearing the story told directly to them, the parents have a greater appreciation of the child's experience.

If the telling is too hard, the therapist can talk for the child. This is an emotionally intense experience. In talking for the child, they are involved in the retelling without the pressure to speak.

When it is too hard for the child to be part of this retelling, the practitioner can talk about the child to the parents. This gives the child a bit of distance as they become a more passive witness to their own story.

This then is the contour of the session.

Talking to: Interspersed with connect and chat and connect and relax, the therapist and child talk together. They explore the experience of the child, guided by the themes that the child presents. The story is co-created. Sometimes, the parents join in, adding information or insights that assist with this co-creation. The therapist might also bring in activities that help the story to emerge – drawing, writing, puppets, sand trays can all be used as part of this act of co-creation. Sometimes, the child needs a den to hide in, so that they can be part of the creative process without being seen.

Talking about: At intervals during the session the therapist will talk about the child to the parents, retelling the story while the child witnesses it. The child might sit with the parents or might prefer to retreat to their den to observe the parents' response.

Talking for: When the therapist judges that the child can tolerate increased emotional intensity while needing help finding the words, they move to 'talking for'. The therapist ensures that it is the child's experience they are conveying and not the story they would like the child to hold.

'Talking for' can also be used when the parents need help to increase their acceptance and empathy for the child. It can guide the parents to find the authentic words the child needs to hear. This needs to be the parents' truth as they experience empathy and acceptance for the child arising out of their witnessing.

> 'Together your parents and I witness your stories. When you find it hard to find the words, I help you.'

An example might be helpful to see how 'talking about' and 'talking for' can work together. Let's revisit Elisha from Chapters 34 and 36.

It is towards the end of the session and the therapist wants to ensure that Elisha experiences Helen and Gail's acceptance. Discovering this story together has been emotionally intense and so the therapist begins by 'talking about' Elisha to Helen and Gail.

Therapist: 'Your daughter has been so brave today. She has let us know how frightened she was when she heard you, Helen, on the phone. It was such a muddle. She thought you were going to have a baby. That was very frightening as she worried that she wouldn't be needed any more.'

(At this point, Elisha joins in, signalling that she is ready to be more active in the retelling.)

Elisha: 'I worried that I wouldn't look after the baby right and then you wouldn't want me any more.'

Therapist: 'That is right, Elisha. I missed out something very important, didn't I? Shall we tell Helen and Gail about how you had to look after your brother when you were little?'

Elisha: 'You tell them.'

Therapist: 'Of course, if it's okay I'll talk for you. Maybe it would feel good to sit between Helen and Gail while I do. (*Elisha moves to sit between her mums.*) Helen, Gail, I'm going to talk for Elisha. Please can you look at your daughter while I do. Elisha may not want to look at you just yet, and that's fine. Elisha, let me know if I get anything wrong or miss anything out.'

Elisha: 'Okay.'

Therapist: 'Mummy Helen and mum Gail, I've been so worried when I heard about the baby. I thought it was going to be your baby, and I was scared that I wouldn't be able to look after the baby right and then you wouldn't want me any more. I tried so hard to look after my brother when he was born. I wanted to keep him quiet while mummy slept, but he kept crying. Mummy was so cross (*turns to Elisha*). How am I doing? Have I missed anything?'

Elisha: 'Mummy sent us away.'

Therapist: 'Ah, yes, that's important. (*Elisha cries quietly, as the therapist continues.*) I tried so hard, but I wasn't good enough. I wanted to be a good girl for mummy. I wanted to look after my brother. He kept crying. Mummy sent us away. You looked after us and my brother stopped crying. I was so frightened that if you had a baby, I wouldn't be able to look after it. Then you wouldn't want me.'

(Elisha is satisfied that nothing has been missed out, so the therapist asks Helen and Gail what they would like to say to Elisha.)

Helen: Oh, sweetheart, of course we won't send you away.

(The therapist is concerned that by Helen moving so quickly to reassurance, Elisha is not experiencing her story being fully heard. As agreed, and practised with the parents, the therapist therefore moves back to 'talk for'. Here

it is used as a way of guiding the parents towards expressing empathy and acceptance.)

Therapist: 'But if I'm really naughty, then you might. I want to be good but sometimes you get cross and then I think you won't want me any more.'

Helen: 'That must be so scary, to think that. I didn't know you had such big worries. All mummies get cross with their children sometimes. I didn't understand how scared it made you feel.'

Gail: 'I'm glad you've let us know, Elisha. I feel so sad that you have such a big worry. I expect we'll get cross from time to time, but we'll remember how scary this is for you. We'll remember to let you know that we're feeling cross but that we'll figure it out together. We don't want you to be alone with these worries.'

(It is nearly time for the session to end. After a final cuddle, the therapist guides them to some connect and relax, helping Elisha to move away from the intensity of the work.)

Within therapy the DDP therapist helps the child to discover the story of their current experience linked, when appropriate, to their past experience. The therapist supports the child in the retelling of this story, so that it is fully witnessed with acceptance and empathy from the therapist and parents.

Emotional connection allows the child to experience safely moving into the vulnerability that is generated by recalling the experience. The support and comfort of the parent(s) provides an experience that is different from what is expected. The child is not abandoned and their belief that they are a bad kid starts to reduce.

IN SEARCH OF A DAUGHTER'S STORY

(I wrote this story as an introduction to story writing in a previous book.[2] Its theme fits well with this chapter and so I repeat it here.)

Once upon a time there were two parents caring for their first child. They were kind and loving and the child, a daughter, had everything her heart desired. She grew in strength, wisdom and beauty but these parents were not content. They wanted to give their child everything she needed, and they feared that there was one thing missing. They had no stories for her.

They did read to her, shared with her the lovely story books written for children of her age, but none of these were created especially for her. They feared that they were letting her down by not finding a story that was hers alone.

One day, their worrying reached a climax; their daughter was beginning to fret as she picked up on her parents' distress. They knew they had to do something. One of the parents decided that he would go out into the world and hunt for her story. He packed a small bag of provisions and with a last look at his partner and their child he set off.

Over the next few weeks, he travelled far and wide searching for her story. He came to many strange and wonderful places, and he saw many people. With each person he met he asked if they knew the story created for his daughter.

These were kind people, who could see the distress in this father's eyes. They searched their minds for the stories they knew, hoping that one of these would be the story he was seeking, but no, the story created especially for his precious daughter remained elusive. He began to

---

2   Golding, K.S. (2014) *Using Stories to Build Bridges with Traumatized Children. Creative Ideas for Therapy, Life Story Work, Direct Work and Parenting.* London: Jessica Kingsley Publishers.

despair. He wanted to get back to his family; but he could not return empty-handed.

At last, tired and foot weary, he entered an inn and ordered a light supper. The inn was very crowded as it was festival time in the town. He squeezed into the only seat remaining at a table already occupied by another man. They sat in companionable silence as each consumed his meal and then they struck up conversation over a final drink.

Soon, as it was never far from his mind, the father told of his quest and wondered if this companion might know where he could find the story he was seeking.

The companion asked him about his daughter. The father told of her intelligence and her beauty. He shared the things that made him and his partner laugh; the little things she might do and say. He shared the struggles of protecting a small child determined to test her independence.

He then told the story of her coming to them as a foundling child and how precious and vulnerable she seemed when she arrived with nothing but a blanket left by some unknown birth mother.

As the sun set on the town the father talked with delight about this daughter who was so close to his heart while his companion listened, nodding occasionally in encouragement. Finally, the father returned to his quest and how it had brought him to this town on this night, but how his heart longed to return to his home and his family.

The companion looked at him with kindness in his eyes. He gently touched the father on the arm and told him: 'Thank you for letting me hear your daughter's story. Go home; they're waiting for you. You've found the story you've been looking for; you need search no more.'

And so, the father returned home understanding at last that his daughter's story had been with him all along.

DDP IN THERAPY

DDP IN THERAPY

Conclusion: DDP Offers Children a Chance to Get Their Future Back

Have you ever held a newborn baby and wondered what their life will be like? What will be their gifts? What will be their challenges? What will the future bring for this little one?

> 'Children are born with potential but not all children fulfil this potential.'

Whether parent, practitioner or both, you know how devastating the impact can be for children born into environments that are developmentally traumatizing.

Children grow up to be parents. Without the quality of parenting that they needed they fail to provide the environments their children need. These children in turn grow up to be parents, and so it continues.

REFLECTION MOMENT

Pause for a moment and remind yourself of some of the impacts of relational traumas.

★ Consider how this impact moves down the generations.

How do we halt this cycle of disadvantage?

Parents are given support, but it is often not enough. They are offered parenting classes, but these do not help with the traumas the parents have experienced.

Sometimes children are moved to foster homes, adoptive homes, residential homes. Sometimes relatives step in to raise these children. These interventions, while often necessary, add another layer of trauma for the children. The loss of their birth family cuts deep. This can lead to challenges for the children and those parenting them.

REFLECTION MOMENT

If you are a person who was impacted by relational traumas as a child:

★ What support did you need?
★ Were there challenges alongside the relational traumas that you needed support for?
★ If you did not experience this impact, imagine being such a person.

Having been interested enough to join me in these explorations, I'm sure you agree that these children, their families and their educators need support to overcome the challenges because of the impact of relational traumas.

This support needs to consider the other difficulties the children have inherited alongside developmental trauma. This might be biological difficulties they have acquired or inherited; difficulties stemming from the impact of living in marginalized or oppressed communities; or difficulties they encounter as they develop such as educational problems, struggles with sexual and gender identity, and managing relationships.

Have you, like me, witnessed the devastating impact on sense of identity that relational traumas and their intersection with other areas of challenge can have on a child?

So often these children feel not good enough. They believe that what has happened to them has been caused by inadequacies in themselves. They are simply bad.

How can they hold hope for their future when they are coping with such a difficult legacy?

'Children who feel that they are bad to the core lose hope for the future.'

If these children are to fulfil their potential, to have their futures returned to them, they deserve well-supported families and schools, approaches that consider the impact of trauma and associated difficulties, and therapies delivered at a time and pace they are ready for.

Dan Hughes recognized this need when he started working with children living in foster care. The traditional support and therapies were not helping the children or their families. He developed dyadic developmental psychotherapy as a way of addressing this problem.

Since those early days, DDP has developed beyond his initial expectations into a therapy, parenting and practice model.

We are still discovering the breadth of help that DDP can offer. We also understand the limitations in terms of cost and time-commitment of long-term therapies. It can also be difficult for parents to be in a place to offer acceptance and empathy to their children.

We are exploring how DDP can combine with other models and approaches to increase the support for children and families. Research is ongoing, which will improve our understanding of what works for whom.

At the beginning of the book, I introduced you to the DDP practice model in its current form. I expect this model will continue to expand. Maybe, in exploring DDP with me you have thought of additions to our model.

This is not the end of the story.

I hope that you are as excited as I am to see how it will develop.

So, let's enjoy one final, whimsical story, inspired by a clear, cold January night in England with Venus shining brightly above a crescent moon.

VENUS LOSES HOPE

Long ago when the solar system was different to today, the planet Venus had her beginning. There were great hopes and expectations for her. It was said that the peoples of Earth would call her the morning and evening 'star' because of how brightly she would shine. Many would marvel at the celestial scene she helped to create in the sky. Sailors and farmers would especially need her light.

Venus had an important role to fulfil.

It was a future Venus eagerly anticipated. She even boasted of it to the other planets. They didn't mind. They each had important roles in the solar system. They didn't begrudge Venus hers.

Moon was especially close to Venus, taking a parental role in her development. Moon was proud that he could help Venus to be what she was born to be.

Venus eagerly awaited her brightening, but the years went by, and she seemed as dark as ever.

'Give it time,' said Moon. 'It will happen. It's meant to be.'

Venus trusted Moon, but years passed with no difference. She began to doubt Moon's words. She fretted, constantly checking to see how bright she was shining. She remained dull, hardly noticeable in the sky. She wondered if she'd done something wrong. Maybe this was her punishment. Maybe it was because she boasted to the other planets. Maybe there was something inside, something bad at the core of her.

Moon told her there was nothing bad about her, but how could he know? Maybe there was a badness he couldn't see, and this was stopping her brightening.

Venus tried being extra good, hoping this would make a difference, but no, she stayed as dull as ever.

She started to get crochety, snapping at the other planets, being bossy with the stars. Now they would see her badness, she thought. Now they would know why she couldn't brighten, but it was hard to stop.

The lovely, gentle Venus, liked by everyone, disappeared and the other planets started to avoid her. Brightening seemed a distant dream, never to be realized.

Moon was worried about Venus and wanted to help. He didn't know what to do but he was sure that she wasn't as bad as she feared. He'd be crotchety too if he couldn't fulfil his purpose. He dearly wanted Venus to become the bright planet she was meant to be.

Sun was wise in lots of matters; Moon decided to consult her. She was sympathetic as he explained the problem. She agreed with Moon that Venus was not a bad planet. She was just young and frightened.

'I've told her that,' said Moon. 'She won't listen to me.'

'Maybe she needs you to listen to her,' suggested Sun. 'Be with her. Let her know you understand. Of course she's afraid, when so much was expected of her. Be with her, Moon, and I'll see if I can find out what the problem is.'

Moon did as Sun suggested. He stayed with Venus. He listened to her worries. He let her know he understood. Venus felt better with Moon's support and did become less crotchety. She still fretted though. What would she do if she could not be a bright light in the sky?

A few months went by as Sun pondered the problem and consulted with other planets. Saturn was especially helpful. His rings had caused problems to some of the minor planets. He wondered if something similar had happened to Venus. Sun wondered what that could have been.

Then one day, all the planets were in a state of excitement. A comet was passing through the solar system. It was only a small one, but it was always a wonder to watch them streak through the sky.

Sun smiled at the planets' excitement and a thought occurred to her. There had been a large comet passing through at the time of Venus' beginning. Might this be the problem? Could the debris in the comet's tail have stopped Venus glowing brightly? If so, would a burst of her sunlight blow the dust away?

They had to wait until Venus's orbit passed close to Sun. Venus could hardly wait. Would this work? She hardly dared to think about it, but a little bit of hope grew inside her.

At last, the day arrived. The planets were excited and lined up in the sky to watch. Moon stayed close to Venus, ready to protect her if needed.

Sun waited for just the right moment. As Venus moved into position, Sun gave a small burst of sunlight to see what would happen. Sure enough, a small amount of dust blew away and Venus looked a little brighter. Sun gave a bigger burst and then another, always checking with Venus that it wasn't too much. Venus was brave. She tolerated as much sunlight as she could before signalling enough.

If planets could breathe, there would have been a collective holding of breath on that day. There was a collective sigh as Sun finished and they all looked at Venus.

The dust was gone, and there was Venus in all her glory. She was the brightest planet in the sky. Moon watched proudly as Venus shone out.

Thanks to Moon's support and Sun's help, Venus had her future back. She shone proudly, bringing extra light to the solar system. On Earth, many sailors navigated safely during dark evenings because of Venus' bright light. Many farmers were comforted by Venus in the sky as they went out in the early morning to tend to their animals.

Venus, the planet, truly had become the evening and morning 'star' for the peoples of Earth.

FINAL REFLECTIONS

Acknowledgements

This book has taken a long time to come together. It started as a lock-down project during the Covid pandemic when the world became quieter, and the act of creation helped me to cope with the sudden changes in our lives that we were all experiencing.

My thanks go to Steve Jones at Jessica Kingsley Publishers, who gave me the original idea to work on. The initial idea changed and grew, and then the world got busy again. Steve helped keep the idea alive and it has been my pleasure to work with him to bring this book to fruition.

I am so grateful to Juliet Young, who embraced this project and has enhanced the book with her illustrations. In working with Juliet, I have realized how much of a word person I am. The visual elements of this book have helped to provide a balance which I would not have achieved on my own.

Within this book, I have wanted to include many different experiences, not all of which are my own lived experience. I am so aware of the responsibility I have when moving outside my own experience. I am grateful to the people I have reached out to who have read some of my stories and guided me in making them true to experiences that are not my own. I thank Ben Hargrave, Julie Hudson, Lily Golding, Shirley Popat, Richard Golding and Kelsey Hampson for their advice.

Thanks also to Chris Barrett for science facts, which I may or may not have followed, and to Alex Barrett for his wisdom in finding the right names for fantasy characters.